• T R O P H I E S •

Practice Book

Grade 6

Harcourt

Orlando   Boston   Dallas   Chicago   San Diego

Visit *The Learning Site!*
www.harcourtschool.com

Printed in the United States of America

ISBN 0-15-323530-6

1 2 3 4 5 6 7 8 9 10 054 10 09 08 07 06 05 04 03 02 01

Contents

TIMELESS TREASURES

Name _____

► Read the Vocabulary Words. Then use the Vocabulary Words to complete the webs.

compliment   enterprising
quality   shrewd
resourceful   inventive
embarrassment

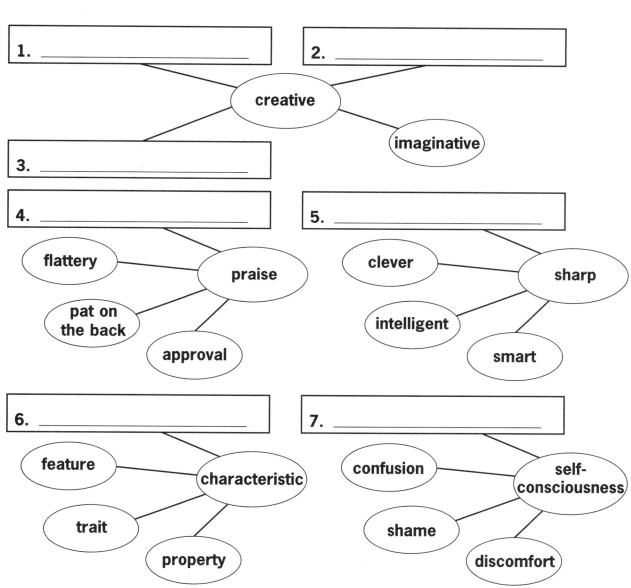

1. _____   2. _____

creative

imaginative

3. _____

4. _____   5. _____

flattery   praise   clever   sharp

pat on
the back   intelligent

approval   smart

6. _____   7. _____

feature   confusion   self-
          characteristic   consciousness

trait   shame

          property   discomfort

1

Name _____

▶ **Read the paragraph. Circle the letter of the best answer to each
question.**

Shelley had promised herself that she would be a good speller this
year. For two years, she had always waited until the Thursday night
before the test to study her spelling words, and she often made
mistakes on the test. This year, the words were longer and
harder. Shelley had a plan that began with writing the words
in a list on Monday and Tuesday, writing each word in a
sentence on Wednesday, and asking Aunt Sue to test her
on Thursday. Last year Shelley had conquered division.
This year, she knew she could conquer spelling.

1 What problem does Shelley have?

  A She is a poor speller.

  B She can't do long division.

  C She doesn't have a plan.

  D She doesn't like Aunt Sue.

💡**Tip**
Find the sentence that says what
Shelley wants to be. How does this
sentence tell what her problem is?

2 What is the theme of the passage?

  F You can improve if you want to.

  G Never make plans.

  H Other people can help you.

  J Spelling is easy for most people.

💡**Tip**
Think about the overall message that
this paragraph communicates.

3 Which word describes Shelley?

  A lazy

  B determined

  C nervous

  D friendly

💡**Tip**
Select the word that describes a
person with a plan to accomplish
something.

© Harcourt

SCHOOL-HOME CONNECTION Have your child
retell a story. Take turns analyzing the narrative
elements of that story (characters, setting, plot,
and theme).

Practice Book
Timeless Treasures

Name _____

▶ **Read the passage. Then write who made each statement. Write *not dialogue* if no one said the words.**

"Don't go in there, please," said Mrs. Green. "My preschool children are napping."

John walked to the next door. "I'm delivering the package to Room 302, Mr. Morales's third-grade class," John said. "I just stopped to see if I could say hi to my little sister."

Just then a head popped out of the door. "Mrs. Green, can you come in?" Mrs. Woo asked.

John stopped and looked at the empty hall. He said softly to himself, "Oh, no! I'm on the wrong floor. No wonder Mrs. Green stopped me. She must have thought I was lost."

1. "I just stopped to see if I could say hi to my little sister." _____

2. "Don't go in there, please." _____

3. Just then a head popped out of the door. _____

4. "Mrs. Green, can you come in?" _____

▶ **Circle the letter of the correct answer.**

5. Mrs. Green teaches _____.

   F third grade

   G sixth grade

   H preschool

6. The last thing John says helps you realize that he feels _____.

   A happy

   B angry

   C foolish

▶ **Write about what John will do next. Include dialogue between him and one other person.**

_____

_____

_____

SCHOOL-HOME CONNECTION Choose a passage from a book that contains dialogue. Ask your child how he or she can tell which character is speaking. Then read the dialogue aloud.

Practice Book
Timeless Treasures

Skill Reminder • **Declarative sentences** make statements and end with a period. • **Interrogative sentences** ask questions and end with a question mark. • **Exclamatory sentences** express strong feeling and end with an exclamation mark. • An **interjection** is a word or group of words that expresses a strong feeling but is not a sentence. It may introduce an exclamatory sentence. Use a comma or an exclamation mark after it.

▶ In the blank, write *declarative*, *interrogative*, *imperative*, or *exclamatory* to identify the type of sentence. Write *interjection* if the sentence starts with one.

1. Imogene was certainly an inventive person. _____

2. Oh! I thought of something to say! _____

3. Why didn't Beth think of that word sooner? _____

4. What kind of compliment is that? _____

5. Speak a little louder. _____

6. Imogene wrote notes to herself on her arm. _____

▶ Rewrite each sentence correctly, using capital letters and end marks. Then identify the type of sentence. Identify interjections.

7. she said some great things

_____

8. gee I wish I'd said that

_____

9. wasn't this a great day

_____

10. Read this card from Albert

_____

 TRY THIS! Reread the first page of "The Best School Year Ever." Find examples of interrogative sentences. Write your examples on a sheet of paper.

Practice Book
Timeless Treasures

Skill Reminder • Short *a* can be spelled *a,* as in *bat.* • Short *e* can be spelled *e,* as in *get.* • Short *i* can be spelled *i,* as in *rip.* • Short *o* can be spelled *o,* as in *not.* • Short *u* can be spelled *u,* as in *fun.*

▶ Fold the paper along the dotted line. As each spelling word is read aloud, write it in the blank. Then unfold your paper, and check your work. Practice spelling any words you missed.

1. _____
2. _____
3. _____
4. _____
5. _____
6. _____
7. _____
8. _____
9. _____
10. _____
11. _____
12. _____
13. _____
14. _____
15. _____
16. _____
17. _____
18. _____
19. _____
20. _____

SPELLING WORDS

1. pledge
2. glasses
3. messages
4. public
5. planet
6. themselves
7. connect
8. guess
9. magic
10. recommend
11. college
12. grabbed
13. compliments
14. optimism
15. success
16. impress
17. solve
18. bronze
19. pulse
20. crumple

Practice Book
Timeless Treasures

© Harcourt

Name _____

▶ **Read the Vocabulary Words. Then write the Vocabulary Word that best completes each sentence.**

novelty	arcade	sulkiness	hilarious
flourish	unaccompanied	vendors	

We visited the shops at the **(1)** _____ after the show. On

the way, **(2)** _____ tried to sell Dad everything from toys to

tortillas. My **(3)** _____ at having to see a movie I didn't want to

see went away as I watched the **(4)** _____ antics of the vendors.

We listened to one violinist play an **(5)** _____ solo. She finished

with a **(6)** _____, sweeping her bow up into the air. Then the

(7) _____ of the market wore off and we went to our old familiar
mall.

▶ **Write the Vocabulary Word that correctly completes each analogy.**

8. *Sing* is to *choirs* as *sell* is to _____.

9. *Sad* is to *sorrowful* as *funny* is to _____.

10. *Colorful* is to *vibrant* as *solo* is to _____.

11. *Young* is to *old* as *ordinary* is to _____.

12. *Car* is to *parking lot* as *store* is to _____.

 TRY THIS! Choose one Vocabulary Word. If the word is a noun, write three adjectives that can describe it. If the word is a verb, write three adverbs that can describe it. If the word is an adverb, write three verbs that can be described by the adverb.

Practice Book
Timeless Treasures

Name _____

▶ **Read the paragraph. Circle the letter of the best answer to each question.**

Music lessons can be beneficial, even to a natural musician. A lot of practice enables a musician to become skilled. A performance in front of an instructor every week can help with stage fright. When a musician plays with little expression, the audience is likely to lose interest in the performance. Proper instruction can help a musician to learn how to make each performance successful.

1 What is the meaning of the word *beneficial*?

A good; helpful

B time-consuming

C harmless

D difficult

Tip
To figure out the meaning of the word *beneficial,* think of the meaning of the root *bene.*

2 Which word does NOT have the same prefix as the word *enables*?

F enclose

G encourage

H endless

J enslave

Tip
Think of what *en-* means in the word *enables.* Then find a word in which *en-* does not have that meaning.

3 What is the root of the word *instruction*?

A in

B struct

C ion

D struction

Tip
Break the word *instruction* into its smallest unit of meaning. After you have identified the prefix and the suffix, the root is left.

© Harcourt

SCHOOL-HOME CONNECTION With your child, search through a newspaper or magazine article for words with prefixes and suffixes. Together, determine the root words. Keep a list and add words as you find them.

Practice Book
Timeless Treasures

Name _____

▶ **Read the paragraphs. Then answer the questions.**

The musician played for more than an hour. She had a blissful look on her face as she listened to the beautiful sound of her piano. When she finished, she smiled with pleasure at the audience. They clapped and cheered loudly, and she blew them kisses.

1. Circle the word that tells the paragraph's mood: happiness   sadness   fear   mystery

2. What words and phrases set the mood? _____

_____

Jason walked slowly down the street. He heard what might have been footsteps behind him, but he was sure it was the wind. The street was dark and he was alone. If he could just get to the corner where there were bright lights, he would feel better.

3. Circle the word that tells the paragraph's mood: happiness   sadness   fear   mystery

4. What words and phrases set the mood? _____

_____

Eloise received a surprise card in the mail. No one had signed the card, and Eloise could not figure out who sent it. She called her friends and relatives, but none of them had sent the card. Eloise thought and thought, but she just could not begin to guess.

5. Circle the word that tells the paragraph's mood: happiness   sadness   fear   mystery

6. What words and phrases set the mood? _____

_____

Marlene watched a war movie. A young couple had just gotten married, but the man went off to war and was soon missing in action. His wife burst into tears when she heard the news, and Marlene felt so bad, she was ready to cry, too.

7. Circle the word that tells the paragraph's mood: happiness   sadness   fear   mystery

8. What words and phrases set the mood? _____

_____

SCHOOL-HOME CONNECTION Have your child make up a story that creates a mood. After he or she tells you the story, guess the mood. Discuss reasons why the story conveyed the particular mood.

8

Practice Book
Timeless Treasures

© Harcourt

Name _____

Skill Reminder   • The **complete subject** includes all the words telling who or what the sentence is about.   • The **simple subject** is the main word or words in the complete subject.

▶ Underline the complete subject and circle the simple subject in each sentence.

1. Eldest Brother needed to make some money.

2. His two brothers suggested playing the violin at Pike Place Market.

3. Many tourists visited the market on weekends.

4. Two musicians gave Eldest Brother an idea.

5. They told Eldest Brother to play at a street fair.

6. A clever juggler was attracting a lot of attention there.

7. A little girl was also playing the violin.

8. She teamed up with Eldest Brother.

▶ Rewrite the following sentences, adding complete subjects. Circle the simple subject in each sentence you write.

9. _____ make money at street fairs in our town.

   _____

   _____

10. _____ wait in line to see exhibits and performers.

    _____

    _____

Name _____

Skill Reminder   • The letters *ai* can spell the long *a* sound in *bait*.   • The letters *ea* can spell the long *e* sound in *meat*. • The letters *igh* can spell the long *i* sound in *sigh*.   • The letters *ough* can spell the long *o* sound in *dough*.

▶ Fold the paper along the dotted line. As each spelling word is read aloud, write it in the blank. Then unfold your paper, and check your work. Practice spelling any words you missed.

1. _____
2. _____
3. _____
4. _____
5. _____
6. _____
7. _____
8. _____
9. _____
10. _____
11. _____
12. _____
13. _____
14. _____
15. _____
16. _____
17. _____
18. _____
19. _____
20. _____

SPELLING WORDS

1. painting
2. leader
3. frightful
4. dough
5. praise
6. reveal
7. slight
8. although
9. defeat
10. remain
11. tightly
12. afraid
13. straighten
14. thorough
15. teammates
16. lightning
17. season
18. breathe
19. mighty
20. retreat

© Harcourt

Practice Book
Timeless Treasures

Name _____

▶ Read the story below, using context clues to determine the meanings of the Vocabulary Words in dark print. Then write each Vocabulary Word next to its definition.

To some people it's just a grubby old ticket stub, but to me it's a **memento** of one of the most exciting days of my life. This is the stub of my ticket to see the Texas Rangers play the Oakland A's on August 22, 1989. It was there that I got to see Nolan Ryan, baseball's all-time strikeout king, record the 5,000th strikeout of his career. Even though most pitchers are past the **peak** of their careers by the time they're 35 years old, Ryan was still mowing down opposing batters at age 42. The Rangers were almost always **favored** to win whenever Ryan pitched, and everybody expected that he might reach strikeout number 5,000 that night.

Excitement was high as players **trotted** to their positions to begin the game, and the fans' frenzy grew as the game went on. Ryan would **glare** at home plate, wind up, and fire a pitch so hard that batters could only wave at it weakly. By the time he struck out Rickey Henderson for number 5,000, we were all on our feet and cheering wildly. I'll never forget that moment, and even though I didn't see any of Ryan's seven no-hitters, I can **console** myself by remembering that I did get to witness that famous 5,000th strikeout. Of course, nobody is **immune** to injury, and Ryan retired four years later with a damaged elbow. What a pitcher he was!

1. _____ considered likely to win

2. _____ protected against

3. _____ something kept or given as a reminder of the past

4. _____ highest level

5. _____ ran, but not too fast

6. _____ comfort

7. _____ stare with hostility

▶ Some of the Vocabulary Words have more than one meaning. Write the word that fits each definition below.

8. _____ the top of a mountain

9. _____ dazzling light

10. _____ treated specially

Practice Book
Timeless Treasures

© Harcourt

Name _____

▶ **Read the paragraph. Circle the letter of the best answer to each question.**

A skilled athlete has a better chance of getting a good job than an athlete with little experience. My cousin has been a track and field star since his first race in junior high. Not only was he the best long jumper, but he was an excellent sprinter and relay racer. As an adult, he displays his medals and trophies at work. Because he is a skilled athlete, he has the job of his dreams.

1 Why might you question the information in the passage?

A because being a skilled athlete doesn't always mean you will get a job

B because it doesn't give any of the athlete's statistics

C because it doesn't name the athlete

D because we don't know how old the author of the passage is

> 💡 **Tip**
> Consider what the passage actually tells you about the cousin's job and why he got it.

2 The passage tries to make you believe in the value of athletics by

F linking it to getting a good job.

G explaining how the cousin got to be good at various events.

H talking about athletic training.

J listing the cousin's awards.

> 💡 **Tip**
> Choose the answer that best matches the main idea of the passage.

3 You know this argument is flawed because

A the author is related to the cousin.

B the author does not discuss how the cousin got his dream job.

C the author doesn't give the cousin's name.

D the author doesn't say how old the cousin is.

> 💡 **Tip**
> Find the choice that suggests that there is a lack of evidence.

SCHOOL-HOME CONNECTION Ask your child to write five positive qualities on index cards, one per card. For example, write *brave* on one card. On the back of each card, write something a *brave* person would do.

Practice Book
Timeless Treasures

© Harcourt

Name _____

▶ **Read the paragraphs. Then answer the questions below. For each question, write one sentence that supports your answer.**

Paragraph A It wasn't until I became a runner that I began to see the world more clearly. Before the summer I started running, it had been an awful school year. I had no friends, I grew a foot every month (or so it seemed), and my clothes never quite seemed to fit. Finally, summer came and a neighbor had to go out of town for a long time. He asked me to take care of his greyhound puppy, who loved to run. That summer I ran through the neighborhood and opened my eyes to my surroundings. I realized that I had a good life ahead of me, despite the drama of the bad school year.

Paragraph B Marie Ellen Sanders became a track star, mainly because of her neighbor's dog. Before she started running, Ms. Sanders seemed content to sit and watch the world go by. She did poorly in school. She had few interests. When she started running, all that changed. She went from dog-running to training at the city parks and then running for her high school track team. Today, Ms. Sanders likes to talk to students and motivates them to run like she did.

1. Which paragraph(s) is an autobiography? _____

_____

2. Which paragraph(s) tells events in time order? _____

_____

3. Which paragraph(s) expresses personal thoughts and feelings? _____

_____

4. Which paragraph(s) is a biography? _____

_____

▶ **Use the information you have written and what you already know to fill in the chart below. Note: Some characteristics belong on both sides of the chart.**

Characteristics of an Autobiography	Characteristics of a Biography

SCHOOL-HOME CONNECTION Have your child write down five to ten events from his or her life on index cards. Then have your child arrange the cards in time order.

13

Name _____

Knots in My
Yo-yo String

Grammar:
Complete and
Simple Predicate

Skill Reminder • The **complete predicate** includes all the words that tell what the subject of the sentence is or does.
• The **simple predicate** is the verb in the complete predicate.

▶ **Underline the complete predicate and circle the simple predicate in each sentence.**

1. The two boys tossed the ball back and forth.

2. They imagined themselves in the stadium.

3. Willie Mays was batting to them.

4. The boy oiled his glove.

5. He pressed a baseball into the

center of the glove.

6. Then he squeezed the glove

into a shoebox.

▶ **Rewrite the following sentences, adding complete predicates.**
Circle the simple predicate in each sentence you write.

7. The boy _____

_____

8. His first sport _____

_____

9. His skills _____

_____

10. Baseball _____

_____

TRY THIS! Look through a magazine or newspaper to find ten sentences that include complete predicates longer than one word. Write your examples on a sheet of paper.

© Harcourt

Name _____

Skill Reminder • The /är/ sound can be spelled *ar*. • The /âr/ sound can be spelled *ear* or *ar*. • The /ôr/ sound can be spelled *oar* or *our*. • The /ûr/ sound can be spelled *or*. • The /ər/ sound can be spelled *er* or *or*.

▶ Fold the paper along the dotted line. As each spelling word is read aloud, write it in the blank. Then unfold your paper, and check your work. Practice spelling any words you missed.

1. _____

2. _____

3. _____

4. _____

5. _____

6. _____

7. _____

8. _____

9. _____

10. _____

11. _____

12. _____

13. _____

14. _____

15. _____

16. _____

17. _____

18. _____

19. _____

20. _____

SPELLING WORDS

1. remark
2. wearing
3. resource
4. words
5. scarce
6. startling
7. hoarse
8. average
9. absurd
10. worst
11. fourteen
12. charms
13. beware
14. fortune
15. southern
16. modern
17. worry
18. rumor
19. memory
20. embark

© Harcourt

Practice Book
Timeless Treasures

Name _____

▶ **Read the Vocabulary Words. Then write the Vocabulary Word that best completes each sentence.**

| fumed | rummaged | exhaustion | reluctantly | flexed | instinct |

1. Tired athletes overcome _____ and other hardships to succeed in their various sports.

2. The tennis players _____ over the bad weather during the tournament.

3. Zachary _____ his muscles, demonstrating his bodybuilding style.

4. Sarah Hall _____ through her sister's closet to find a pair of shoes, which she wore in the race.

5. Chess champion Scotty Dale took up the game _____ last year when a broken leg kept him off his feet for several weeks.

6. Almost blinded by a sudden shower, football player David Rosales relied on

_____ to help him kick the game-winning field goal.

▶ **Write the Vocabulary Word that fits best in each word group.**

7. looked, hunted, _____

8. tiredness, fatigue, _____

9. griped, raged, _____

10. hesitantly, unenthusiastically, _____

11. tensed, stretched, _____

12. sense, feeling, _____

TRY THIS! Think about something that you do only reluctantly. Write a few sentences about it, using some of the Vocabulary Words.

© Harcourt

Practice Book
Timeless Treasures

Name _____

▶ **Read the paragraph. Then read the questions. Circle the letter of the best answer to each question.**

No one paid attention to the new girl, Erin. She didn't talk much, and she kept to herself at lunch. Then one morning a cartoon of Ms. Gerber's sixth-grade class showed up on the chalkboard. The artist had drawn each student and had somehow caught each one's personality. Who had done the drawing? Later that day, Erin was called to the front of the class to read her report. On the way up, some papers fell out of her folder. When Ms. Gerber saw them, she laughed. "Well, I guess we know who our artist is!" There in Erin's hand were sketches of the class hard at work. "Maybe you can help do sets for the class play," Juan said to her.

1 What is the problem in this story?

  A Ms. Gerber and the class don't know who did a drawing of them.

  B The class doesn't know how to make the new student feel at home.

  C The new student can't keep up with the work.

  D The class needs someone to do the sets for the class play.

> **Tip**
> To find the problem, look for the sentence that states the question everyone wanted answered.

2 How is the problem resolved?

  F Erin drops additional drawings she has done.

  G Erin admits that she did the drawing.

  H Ms. Gerber demands to know who did the drawing.

  J Juan puts out a call for a set designer.

> **Tip**
> Remember that the resolution is the way the problem is solved.

3 Why was Erin so quiet?

  A She was unfriendly and mean.

  B She was quietly studying her classmates.

  C She was homesick.

  D She wanted to star in the play.

> **Tip**
> The answer to this question is not directly stated. You need to make an inference about Erin's behavior. Review the content of the story.

© Harcourt

SCHOOL-HOME CONNECTION Have your child write a paragraph that follows up on what happens in the story. What does Erin do? How does her personality change, if at all?

Practice Book
Timeless Treasures

Skill Reminder • **A compound subject** is two or more subjects that have the same predicate, usually joined by the conjunction *and* or *or.* • **A compound predicate** is two or more predicates that have the same subject, usually joined by a conjunction such as *and, but,* or *or.*

▶ Underline the compound subject or predicate in each sentence, and circle the conjunction that joins its parts. Write *compound subject* or *compound predicate*, depending on what you underline.

1. Strength and a good eye are important in playing marbles. _____

2. A good thumb or a sharp eye is not enough by itself. _____

3. Lupe sat and listened to her brother. _____

4. She ate dinner but said nothing about her plans. _____

5. An oval in the dirt and the four marbles inside it
   formed the target. _____

6. Dust blew in her eyes and blinded her. _____

7. The shooter bounced, rolled on, and hit a marble. _____

8. Lupe's parents, her brother, and Alfonso encouraged her. _____

▶ Rewrite the following sentences, adding a compound subject or a compound predicate as needed. Make sure one sentence includes either three subjects or three predicates.

9. _____ were needed.

   _____

10. Lupe _____ .

   _____

TRY THIS! Write a sentence about the day's activities that has both a compound subject and a compound predicate. Identify the subjects and predicates.

Name _____

Skill Reminder • The short *i* sound can be spelled *ui* or *y*.
• The short *u* sound can be spelled *o*. • The long *a* sound can be spelled *ea*, *eigh*, or *ei*.

▶ Fold the paper along the dotted line. As each spelling word is read aloud, write it in the blank. Then unfold your paper, and check your work. Practice spelling any words you missed.

1. _____
2. _____
3. _____
4. _____
5. _____
6. _____
7. _____
8. _____
9. _____
10. _____
11. _____
12. _____
13. _____
14. _____
15. _____
16. _____
17. _____
18. _____
19. _____
20. _____

SPELLING WORDS

1. guilty
2. myth
3. brother
4. breaking
5. eighth
6. system
7. neighborly
8. honey
9. among
10. sleigh
11. reign
12. symbol
13. circuit
14. guitar
15. symptoms
16. biscuits
17. ton
18. another
19. veil
20. vein

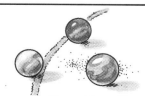

Practice Book
Timeless Treasures

Name _____

▶ **Read the Vocabulary Words. Then write the Vocabulary Word that best completes each sentence in the city council meeting schedule.**

violations	**issue**	**agenda**	**funding**
ordinance	**effective**	**postpone**	

**Summerville City Council
Meeting of April 28, 7:30 P.M.**

1. The secretary reads the _____ listing the items to be discussed at this evening's meeting.
2. The treasurer presents the ideas for _____ street repairs without raising taxes.
3. The council hears speakers in favor of an _____ that would prevent people from keeping horses within the city limits.
4. The council decides whether to vote on the horse question now or to

   _____ the vote until later.

5. The council discusses the _____ of what to do about noise from the airport.
6. The council hears complaints regarding dog owners' _____ of the city leash law.
7. The mayor calls for ideas about ways to make the city's crime-prevention efforts

   more _____ .

▶ **Write the Vocabulary Word with nearly the same meaning as each word below.**

8. delay _____
9. law _____
10. schedule _____
11. financing _____
12. useful _____

Practice Book
Timeless Treasures

© Harcourt

Name _____

▶ **Read the paragraph. Circle the letter of the best answer to each question.**

A city government is responsible for the welfare of all the people who live in the city. It must represent people with different opinions. It must represent the homeless. It must represent youthful and older residents. A city council meeting is a time for interaction among residents. Such meetings are an essential part of a democracy. At a meeting, residents might call for an election of new members. They might discuss the need for better public transportation. Any reasonable issue may become a topic for discussion. Whenever people feel welcome at their city government meetings, democracy works!

1 What is the meaning of *interaction*?

A action or movement between people

B no action on an issue

C two people having an argument

D two people laughing together

> **Tip**
> To answer this question, think of what the prefix *inter-* means.

2 What does the prefix *trans-* in transportation mean?

F too many or excessive

G lack of or not enough

H across or through

J state of being

> **Tip**
> Find the sentence with *transportation*. Remember what the prefix *trans-* means.

3 What is the relationship between the suffix *-ful* and the suffix *-less*?

A They have the same meaning.

B They have opposite meanings.

C Both mean "not."

D Neither one changes the meaning of a root.

> **Tip**
> Find a word with each suffix in the passage. Think about how the meanings are related.

© Harcourt

SCHOOL-HOME CONNECTION Have your child write the prefix *re-* on an index card. Then write another five words. Add the prefix *re-* to each word. Discuss how the prefix *re-* changes the meaning of the words.

Practice Book
Timeless Treasures

Skill Reminder	• **A simple sentence** expresses one complete thought. • **A compound sentence** is made up of two or more simple sentences. • Simple sentences may be joined by a comma and a conjunction such as *and, but,* or *or,* or by a semicolon.

▶ **Combine the simple sentences into compound sentences, using the conjunction suggested in parentheses ( ) and adding commas where needed.**

1. One vote was taken on a violation. The decision was postponed. **(but)**

_____

_____

2. The two students from the school were called on. Linda Gold was first to speak. **(and)**

_____

_____

3. Linda spoke into the microphone. Her voice sounded very snooty. **(and)**

_____

_____

4. The council called on Sweeby. He had only four minutes to speak. **(but)**

_____

_____

5. Five members voted against a garden. One voted for it. Three did not vote at all. **(and)**

_____

_____

▶ **Rewrite each compound sentence below, adding commas and conjunctions, or semicolons, as needed.**

6. Darnell took a deep breath Tamika had tears in her eyes. _____

_____

7. Darnell is a good writer he should write more articles. _____

_____

© Harcourt

Skill Reminder • The saying "*i* before *e* except after *c*" will usually help you spell words with *ei* or *ie*. • Exceptions include *neither, leisure,* and *seize.*

▶ Fold the paper along the dotted line. As each spelling word is read aloud, write it in the blank. Then unfold your paper, and check your work. Practice spelling any words you missed.

1. _____
2. _____
3. _____
4. _____
5. _____
6. _____
7. _____
8. _____
9. _____
10. _____
11. _____
12. _____
13. _____
14. _____
15. _____
16. _____
17. _____
18. _____
19. _____
20. _____

SPELLING WORDS

1. neither
2. friendship
3. fierce
4. thieves
5. foreign
6. girlfriend
7. received
8. relief
9. seize
10. movie
11. yield
12. pierce
13. high-ceilinged
14. achieve
15. leisure
16. briefcase
17. height
18. grief
19. hygiene
20. niece

© Harcourt

Name _____

▶ **Read the letter below, using context clues to determine the meanings of the boldfaced Vocabulary Words. Then write each Vocabulary Word next to its definition.**

Dear Wendy,

What an amazing city Copenhagen is! Last night we went to Tivoli Gardens. Dad was **exasperated** by the traffic on the confusing city streets, but once we were in the gardens, he couldn't feel annoyed any longer. Listening to an orchestra play **soothingly** helped his nerves, too. We wanted to eat dinner at the nice restaurant overlooking Tivoli Lake, but Dad was **unwavering** in his opinion that it would be too expensive. I offered some bread to the ducks that were swimming in the lake, but I guess they had already eaten. They just swam away **disdainfully.** Tivoli is so beautiful that it's hard to believe that German **occupation** troops burned part of it during World War II. How could anyone act so **belligerently** in such a peaceful place? I'll bring you some pictures of the famous Tivoli fireworks!

Your friend,
Stephanie

1. _____ scornfully

2. _____ irritated almost to the point of being angry

3. _____ military forces that take and hold a land

4. _____ in a warlike manner

5. _____ not changing

6. _____ in a way that has a calming effect

▶ **Write the Vocabulary Word that means the opposite of each word below.**

7. peacefully _____

8. irritatingly _____

9. respectfully _____

10. indecisive _____

TRY THIS! What are some things that make you feel *exasperated*? Write about one thing, using at least two Vocabulary Words.

Practice Book
Timeless Treasures

© Harcourt

Name _____

▶ **Read the paragraph. Circle the letter of the best answer to each question.**

To win the speed-skating medal, Kari needs racing skates, but her father can't afford to buy them. Her father sells large blocks of ice cut from Copenhagen's lakes and ponds. The winter temperature has been so mild, however, that even the ponds haven't frozen. As a result, the family has no money for skates. Although Kari's aunt lends her a pair of ice skates, Kari can find nowhere to practice. The ponds aren't safe and the ice rink is too expensive. Kari enters the race but comes in fifth.

1 What element of the setting most influences the action in this paragraph?

   A Kari's aunt lends her skates

   B the city of Copenhagen

   C the mild temperature

   D Kari's father's anger

> 💡 **Tip**
> Think about what happens in the paragraph, and choose the answer that has the greatest effect on the action.

2 Once Kari has racing skates, what conflict does she face?

   F Kari's aunt expects a thank-you note.

   G Kari dislikes the skates' color.

   H Kari's father disapproves of the time Kari spends practicing.

   J She is not able to find a suitable place to practice.

> 💡 **Tip**
> Find the place in the paragraph where Kari gets the ice skates. What difficulty does she face after?

3 How does the setting influence what happens at the end?

   A Because the parks are full, Kari can't practice.

   B Because of the warm weather, Kari misses her chance for a medal.

   C Because her family lives in Copenhagen, Kari is a good skater.

   D Because Kari catches a cold, she can't race.

> 💡 **Tip**
> Which answer choice shows the closest connection between the setting and the end of the story?

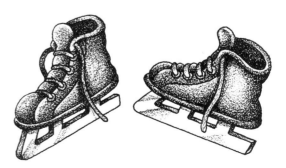

SCHOOL-HOME CONNECTION With your child, look for a television or newspaper story in which setting is important. Have your child explain how the outcome might be different if the story had occurred in a different time or place.

25

Practice Book
Timeless Treasures

Name _____

▶ **Read the questions. Write your answers on the lines.**

1. A red heart is a traditional symbol for what strong emotion? _____

   Give examples to support your answer. _____

   _____

   _____

2. Why does water often symbolize purity? _____

   _____

3. Which season of the year is sometimes a symbol of birth? _____

   Why? _____

4. Doves are traditional symbols of peace. What bird has become a symbol of war,

   and why? _____

   _____

5. Why might the sun represent happiness? _____

   _____

▶ **Match each item below with the quality it symbolizes in "Number the Stars."**
   Write your answer on the line.

_____ 6. dark curls

_____ 7. Tivoli Gardens

_____ 8. the Star of David necklace

a. happy, carefree days

b. an older sister—and a new
   family member

c. a special bond between Ellen
   and Annemarie

 SCHOOL-HOME CONNECTION Help your child
research the symbol of the United States, Uncle
Sam. Find out when he first appeared, why he is
dressed as he is, and what he symbolizes.

26

Practice Book
Timeless Treasures

© Harcourt

Name _____

Skill Reminder • **A clause** is a group of words that contains a subject and a predicate. • **A complex sentence** contains an independent clause and a dependent clause. • **Independent clauses** can stand alone. **Dependent**, or **subordinate**, clauses can not.

▶ **In these complex sentences, underline the independent clauses once and the dependent clauses twice. Circle the conjunction that introduces the dependent clause.**

   1. The girls whispered to each other because they were worried.

   2. Ellen remembered the time when Lise died.

   3. It was raining when Ellen's mother told her about the accident.

   4. If it had not been raining, the car might not have hit Lise.

▶ **Combine the two clauses in each item into one sentence, using the subordinating conjunction in parentheses ( ).**

   5. Ellen's father wanted her to be a teacher. Ellen wanted to go to

   acting school. **(although)** _____

   _____

   _____

   6. Annemarie had not seen Lise's things. Her parents had packed them away.

   (since) _____

   _____

   _____

TRY THIS! Suppose that you were Ellen. Write an eight- or ten-sentence journal entry describing how you felt. Include five sentences with both dependent and independent clauses.

© Harcourt

Name _____

Skill Reminder • The /ər/ sound can be spelled *er*. • The /ən/ sound can be spelled *an* or *en*. • The /əl/ sound can be spelled *al*.

▶ Fold the paper along the dotted line. As each spelling word is read aloud, write it in the blank. Then unfold your paper, and check your work. Practice spelling any words you missed.

1. _____

2. _____

3. _____

4. _____

5. _____

6. _____

7. _____

8. _____

9. _____

10. _____

11. _____

12. _____

13. _____

14. _____

15. _____

16. _____

17. _____

18. _____

19. _____

20. _____

SPELLING WORDS

1. shoulder
2. Roman
3. mental
4. frighten
5. feather
6. individual
7. anger
8. original
9. German
10. dozen
11. hunger
12. musical
13. political
14. citizen
15. oxygen
16. quarter
17. manual
18. computer
19. terror
20. medical

© Harcourt

Practice Book
Timeless Treasures

Name _____

▶ **Read the Vocabulary Words. Then write the Voacabulary Word that best completes each sentence in the newspaper article.**

compulsion	waver	engulf
wailed	disbelief	anguish
expanse		

Lost Child Found Safe

The young boy who was reported lost in the huge **(1)** _____ of forest has been found safe. Charlie's sister, Sara, and her friend, Joe, located

Charlie after their **(2)** _____ to continue the search led them to

the lost child. "I had never felt so much **(3)** _____ and distress

as I did while Charlie was lost," Sara said later. She looked calm, but her voice began

to **(4)** _____ unsteadily as she spoke. "The forest is big enough

to **(5)** _____ a whole army. We had just about given up on finding

him, so for a moment we felt **(6)** _____ when we heard him crying.

As he cried and **(7)** _____, we followed the sound, and there he was."

▶ **Write the Vocabulary Word that fits best in each word group.**

8. agony, misery, _____   11. spread, range, _____

9. wobble, flutter, _____   12. cried, screamed, _____

10. drive, urge, _____

TRY THIS! Think of a time when someone you know was lost. Tell what happened, using as many Vocabulary Words as possible.

Practice Book
Timeless Treasures

Name _____

▶ **Read the paragraph. Then circle the letter of the best answer to each question.**

Lynn and Gregory set out together on a hike, but Lynn soon took the lead. When Lynn was halfway across the route, she began to wonder how Gregory, who was about one hundred feet behind her, was doing. Turning to look at him, she suddenly fell into deep snow. She struggled to get out of the drift, thinking to herself that she couldn't afford to waste any energy. For a few seconds she lay there, motionless. She realized that her best plan was probably to wait for Gregory to catch up with her. She tried not to panic.

1 Who is the narrator in this paragraph?

A Gregory

B Lynn

C the author

D There is no narrator.

💡 **Tip**
Think about whether an "I"—that is, someone in the story—tells the story.

2 What point of view is used in the paragraph?

F first person

G third person omniscient

H third person limited

J second person

💡 **Tip**
Remember that an omniscient narrator knows and tells what a character is thinking.

3 The author used this point of view in order to

A get into the mind of a character.

B keep you in suspense about what characters are thinking.

C tell about himself or herself.

D none of the above

💡 **Tip**
What happens when a writer uses the point of view you chose in question 2?

© Harcourt

SCHOOL-HOME CONNECTION With your child, determine the point of view of a story that he or she has read. See how many sentences your child needs to read in the opening paragraph of a story before identifying its point of view.

30

Practice Book
Timeless Treasures

HOMEWORK
The Summer of the Swans
Sequential Structure

▶ **Read the passage. Then answer the questions that follow.**

At three o'clock, Mrs. Simon pulled into the Myers' Market parking lot. "Let's see," she thought, looking at her list, "I need laundry soap, and the kids need cereal." She quickly got a shopping cart, filled it, and checked out. Then she drove to the cleaners.

By four o'clock she was parked outside Gene's Bait Shop. She tooted the horn a couple of times, but Alex, her older boy, didn't appear. She waited impatiently for a few minutes, and then began to wonder. It *was* at four o'clock that he was to meet her, wasn't it?

Mrs. Simon thought back to six o'clock that morning. Alex, though half asleep, was eager to try out his new fishing rod. Mrs. Simon dropped him off at the bait shop. "I'll be back for you at four o'clock sharp. Okay?" "Okay, Mom," he said, running toward the dock.

It was nearly four-thirty. Where was Alex?

1. What is the first place Mrs. Simon visits?

_____

2. Where does she go next, and how does she get there?

_____

_____

3. What is the final setting of the passage? _____

4. Why does Mrs. Simon go there? _____

_____

5. What is the setting—time and place—of the flashback? _____

_____

6. Which sentence takes you back to the latest time in the story? _____

_____

Practice Book
Timeless Treasures

© Harcourt

The Summer of
the Swans

Grammar:
Compound-
Complex
Sentences

Skill Reminder | A **compound-complex sentence** contains two
or more independent clauses and one or more dependent clauses.

▶ **Underline the dependent clause in each sentence once.
Then underline each independent clause twice.**

1. Charlie was lost, and Sara and Joe were climbing the hill

   because they needed to see the whole valley.

2. As soon as Sara got to the top, she could hear

   Charlie's cries, but Charlie was nowhere in sight.

3. Joe reached the top, and both he and Sara called out to Charlie as they looked

   frantically to spot him.

4. Charlie had not been able to find the path where they had been walking, so he began

   to panic.

▶ **Rewrite each sentence, following the directions in parentheses ( ).**

5. Joe kept climbing, and he soon caught up with Sara. (**Add a dependent clause.**)

   _____

   _____

6. Sara remembered other times when Charlie had gotten lost. (**Add an independent
   clause.**)

   _____

   _____

7. After Sara fell, Joe helped her get up. (**Add an independent clause.**)

   _____

   _____

8. Sara spotted the ravine, and she heard Charlie's screams. (**Add a dependent clause.**)

   _____

   _____

Name _____

Skill Reminder **Homophones** are pairs of words that have the
same pronunciation but different spellings and meanings.

▶ Fold the paper along the dotted line. As each spelling word is read aloud, write it
in the blank. Then unfold your paper, and check your work. Practice spelling any
words you missed.

1. _____

2. _____

3. _____

4. _____

5. _____

6. _____

7. _____

8. _____

9. _____

10. _____

11. _____

12. _____

13. _____

14. _____

15. _____

16. _____

17. _____

18. _____

19. _____

20. _____

SPELLING WORDS

1. there
2. their
3. raise
4. aloud
5. hole
6. through
7. sent
8. raze
9. threw
10. whole
11. scent
12. allowed
13. principal
14. course
15. principle
16. coarse
17. dual
18. flare
19. flair
20. duel

Practice Book
Timeless Treasures

Name _____

▶ Read the tall tale below, using context clues to determine the meaning of each boldfaced Vocabulary Word. Then write each Vocabulary Word next to its definition.

Now, some folks are always accusing me of spinning **yarns,** but I promise you, cross my heart, that this story is true. Last week I was out in the woods behind my cabin, splitting logs for a new fence. I had my new axe with the orange handle to help me do the job. My dog was **romping** and playing around my feet when all of a sudden he sat up real still and then ran to the cabin. I looked up just in time to see the biggest rabbit I ever saw **charging** from behind a bush. That rabbit stopped one big hop away from me, looked me straight in the eye—his eyes were level with mine—and before I knew it, he was **lunging** right at me! Well, I was so **frantic** that I dropped my axe. As it turns out, that was a good thing to do, because the rabbit **pounced** on that orange-handled axe, picked it up with his big teeth, and dashed off into the woods. I reckon he thought it was a giant carrot!

1. _____ making a quick forward movement

2. _____ swooped down suddenly onto something

3. _____ adventure stories, especially those that are not true

4. _____ wildly excited or upset

5. _____ rushing forward violently; attacking

6. _____ playing in a lively, noisy way

▶ Write the Vocabulary Word that best matches each description.

7. an angry moose rushing out of the woods _____

8. a woman who just lost her purse _____

9. children running and playing in the park _____

10. a cat that jumped on a ball of yarn _____

TRY THIS!

Write your own *yarn.* See if you can use all of the Vocabulary Words in your story.

Name _____

▶ **Read the paragraph. Then circle the letter of the best answer to each question.**

The first Saturday of each two-week camp session, a counselor and six campers hike to the top of Little Bear Mountain to see the sunrise. Twenty years ago the mountain deserved its name, but those days are long gone. The only bear that lives in these mountains now is a performing bear that escaped from a traveling circus. Today's glorious sunrise so delights the campers that they break out in applause. A large black bear emerges from the trees, stands on its hind legs, and begins dancing, as if on cue.

1 What is the best paraphrase of the second sentence?

A Twenty years ago the mountain was smaller, but it has grown.

B Many bears lived on the mountain twenty years ago, but no bears have lived there in years.

C Little Bear Mountain got its name from bears that lived on it.

D Only one bear lives on the mountain now.

💡 Tip
Think about the meaning of "long gone" and about why the mountain once "deserved its name."

2 What is the best paraphrase of the last sentence?

F The clapping is a signal to the black bear that it is time to perform.

G Before the clapping ends, the bear starts dancing.

H The dancing bear signals the campers that it is time to return to camp.

J The bear is so lonely for company that it appears at the first sound it hears.

💡 Tip
Eliminate answers that cannot be found in the paragraph.

3 What is the best summary of the paragraph?

A One should always be prepared for any emergency.

B A circus bear is persuaded to perform when campers applaud him loudly.

C Six campers and a counselor hike to the top of a mountain to see a sunrise and encounter a dancing bear.

D Wild animals, such as bears, can appear in places that seem to be safe.

💡 Tip
A summary is different from a moral or a theme.

SCHOOL-HOME CONNECTION With your child, watch a half-hour television program. Working separately, summarize the program in one or two sentences. Compare the summaries. Whose summary is shorter? Whose is more accurate?

Practice Book
Timeless Treasures

Name _____

▶ **Read the passage. Then answer the questions.**

Jed and Tonio ride rapidly into the mouth of a mine. While Jed removes the heavy saddle bags from the worn-out horses, Tonio ties the reins to an old wooden gate. As the horses move nervously, the gate squeaks. Jed lights a small lantern, then says, "The way out is that way. I'll carry the saddle bags. Let's get out of here fast. We can't let that Texas Ranger find our trail." Neither man notices the small dust cloud near the bottom of the hill.

As they step cautiously through the passage, Jed hears thunder as well as quiet steps and the squeaking of the gate. "Those horses aren't going to like a storm," he mutters to himself. The two men move deeper into the mine. Jed flashes the lantern around and warns Tonio, "Watch your footing as we go around that big rock. There's a drop-off." As he starts around the rock, he hears a cry and a clattering noise. Tonio is lying on his back, moaning. "I can't move," he cries.

1. What does the last sentence of paragraph 1 foreshadow? _____

_____

2. In paragraph 2, which sentences foreshadow what will happen to Tonio? _____

_____

3. Name two details that create suspense in the story. Explain how they create suspense.

_____

_____

_____

4. Explain how you think this story will end. Use the foreshadowing clues in the story in

your answer. _____

_____

_____

SCHOOL-HOME CONNECTION Help your child
write a paragraph to end the story. Use some of
the clues that foreshadow how the story will end.

36

Practice Book
Timeless Treasures

© Harcourt

Name _____

Skill Reminder • A **common noun** names any person, place, thing, or idea. A common noun begins with a lowercase letter.
• A **proper noun** names a specific person, place, or thing. All important words in proper nouns begin with capital letters.
• Begin the **abbreviation** for a proper noun with a capital letter. End most abbreviations with periods.

▶ Underline common nouns once and proper nouns twice.

1. Travis was working down by the creek.

2. He was splitting a log.

3. He would make a split, and then he would pound a wedge in.

4. Just before sundown, Travis heard Little Arliss scream.

5. Mama came running down toward Birdsong Creek.

▶ Write the abbreviation of each noun. Use a dictionary if you need to.

6. foot _____   **11.** yard _____

7. mile _____   **12.** street _____

8. avenue _____   **13.** Friday _____

9. February _____   **14.** Doctor _____

10. Mister _____   **15.** Incorporated _____

TRY THIS! You are a well-known expert on rare insects. Write a paragraph about a new species of insect that you have just discovered. Describe the insect's size, weight, and appearance, and tell where you found it. Use abbreviations and proper nouns.

Name _____

Skill Reminder **Some words come from the names of people or places.**

▶ Fold the paper along the dotted line. As each spelling word is read aloud, write it in the blank. Then unfold your paper, and check your work. Practice spelling any words you missed.

1. _____
2. _____
3. _____
4. _____
5. _____
6. _____
7. _____
8. _____
9. _____
10. _____
11. _____
12. _____
13. _____
14. _____
15. _____
16. _____
17. _____
18. _____
19. _____
20. _____

SPELLING WORDS

1. watt
2. braille
3. sandwich
4. tangerine
5. saxophone
6. leotard
7. frankfurter
8. diesel
9. denim
10. mercury
11. Fahrenheit
12. atlas
13. Celsius
14. odyssey
15. tuxedo
16. limousine
17. china
18. attic
19. volt
20. cereal

Practice Book
Timeless Treasures

38

Name _____

▶ Read the Vocabulary Words. Then use the Vocabulary Words to complete the webs.

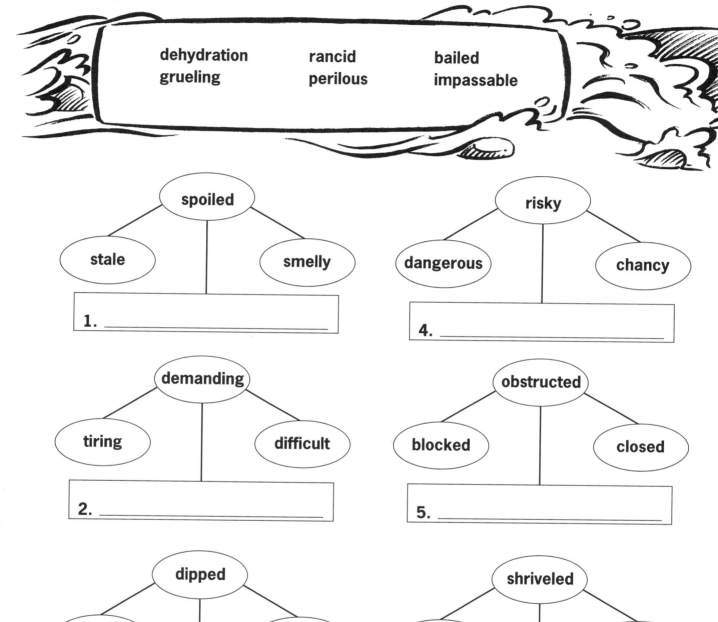

| dehydration | rancid | bailed |
| grueling | perilous | impassable |

spoiled
stale smelly

1. _____

risky
dangerous chancy

4. _____

demanding
tiring difficult

2. _____

obstructed
blocked closed

5. _____

dipped
scooped ladled

3. _____

shriveled
dried up parched

6. _____

TRY THIS! Write three sentences about what it would be like to climb a mountain during a storm. Use as many of the Vocabulary Words as you can.

Practice Book
Timeless Treasures

Name _____

HOMEWORK
Trapped by
the Ice!
Literary Devices:
Figurative
Language
TEST PREP

▶ **Read the following paragraph. Then circle the letter of the best answer to each question.**

Dennis stayed at a resort at a time of the year when the sun smiles only a few hours a day and skiers can find themselves in several kinds of danger. Coming down the slopes one morning, Dennis heard a frightening sound. "Avalanche!" he thought, and skied under an overhanging rock. As the avalanche's speed increased, it became a roaring lion, plunging and raging down the hill. Huddled under the rock, Dennis realized he was not alone. He was sharing the cramped space with a frightened, hissing lynx, whose claws flashed like daggers toward Dennis's face.

1 In the first sentence, "when the sun smiles" is an example of

💡 Tip
What is unusual about this statement?

A narrator

B metaphor

C simile

D personification

2 Which of the following is a metaphor?

💡 Tip
Eliminate answers that do not use figurative language.

F "Avalanche!" he thought.

G skied under an overhanging rock

H it became a roaring lion

J plunging and raging down the hill

3 The figurative language in the last sentence is an example of

💡 Tip
Identify the language that goes beyond an exact description.

A metaphor

B personification

C simile

D theme

SCHOOL-HOME CONNECTION With your child, create several similes and metaphors describing people you both know.

40

Practice Book
Timeless Treasures

© Harcourt

Name _____

Skill Reminder • A **singular noun** names one person, place, thing, or idea. • A **plural noun** names more than one person, place, thing, or idea.

▶ **List each singular noun in the first column and each plural noun in the second column.**

	Singular	Plural
1. Five men fit into the boat.	_____	_____
2. Huge waves battered the hull.	_____	_____
3. A rock with sharp edges could be dangerous.	_____	_____
4. There were several islands in the frigid sea.	_____	_____
5. The winds caused constant peril.	_____	_____

▶ **Rewrite each sentence, using the correct plural form of the nouns in parentheses ( ).**

6. Hunger and terrible weather were the main **(enemy)** of the **(explorer)**.

_____

_____

7. Going thirty **(hour)** without sleep could cause exhaustion or even **(illness)**.

_____

_____

8. Were the **(reward)** of the trip worth all the **(difficulty)**? _____

_____

TRY THIS! Make a family tree or a "friend tree" on a large sheet of paper. Draw a box for yourself connected to other boxes for your family members or friends. In each box, write the person's name, along with things they have one of, two of, and many of. For example: "Jose has one cat, two puppies, and many fish."

Practice Book
Timeless Treasures

Skill Reminder **To determine the correct spelling of easily
confused words, pronounce each word carefully and think about
how it is used in a sentence.**

▶ Fold the paper along the dotted line. As each spelling word is read aloud, write it
in the blank. Then unfold your paper, and check your work. Practice spelling any
words you missed.

1. _____

2. _____

3. _____

4. _____

5. _____

6. _____

7. _____

8. _____

9. _____

10. _____

11. _____

12. _____

13. _____

14. _____

15. _____

16. _____

17. _____

18. _____

19. _____

20. _____

SPELLING WORDS

1. effect
2. angel
3. desert
4. older
5. dessert
6. adopt
7. decent
8. affect
9. angle
10. elder
11. descent
12. adapt
13. broad
14. device
15. personal
16. board
17. devise
18. access
19. personnel
20. excess

© Harcourt

Practice Book
Timeless Treasures

Name _____

▶ **Write the Vocabulary Word that best completes each newspaper headline.**

reservoirs awed levees
floodplain yearned crested
seeping

1. Farms on Mississippi _____ Threatened as Rains Continue

2. Volunteers Rush to Raise _____ at Riverbanks

3. _____ Holding Town's Water Supply Are Full

4. Water _____ Through Sand May Break Levee

5. City Safe; River _____ at 32 Feet

6. Townspeople _____ by Hard Work of Strangers

7. Families _____ to Return to Farms

▶ **Use Vocabulary Words to answer the following questions.**

8. Which word is a compound? _____

9. Which two words are plural? _____

10. Which three words are past-tense verbs? _____

TRY THIS! Write a newspaper story to go with one of the headlines on this page. Use as many Vocabulary Words as you can.

Practice Book
Timeless Treasures

Name _____

▶ **Read the paragraph. Circle the letter of the best answer to each question.**

North America is the habitat of several categories of bears, including black bears, brown bears like the grizzly and the Kodiak, and polar bears. Some bears live in forested areas, while others roam the coasts and islands of Alaska. Black bears are dwarfed by their brown and polar bear relatives. Adult black bears often stand five to six feet tall and weigh 200-600 pounds; adult Kodiaks and polar bears may grow to be over nine feet tall and weigh more than 1,500 pounds. Although black bears can be tamed, all bears should be considered dangerous, especially as they age.

1 What is the best paraphrase of sentence 1?

A Black bears, grizzlies and Kodiaks, and polar bears live in North America.

B Many bears make their home in North America.

C More brown bears live in North America than black or polar bears.

D Grizzly and Kodiak bears live in permanent homes.

> **Tip**
> Which answer choice includes all the information in sentence 1?

2 What is the best paraphrase of the third sentence?

F Many black bears are dwarfs.

G Brown and polar bears are larger than black bears.

H Compared to other animals, brown bears are small.

J The black bear has relatives.

> **Tip**
> A paraphrase often rearranges and restates the information in a sentence.

3 What is the best summary of the paragraph?

A Bears are not to be trusted around small children.

B Black, brown, or polar, North American bears are wonderful hunters.

C Bears can be both entertaining and dangerous, especially as they age.

D North American bears vary in appearance and habitat, but all can be dangerous.

> **Tip**
> Eliminate answers that cannot be found in the passage.

SCHOOL-HOME CONNECTION What kinds of wild animals live in your area? (A wild animal is any animal that is not a pet.) With your child, discuss what you know about these animals. Then take turns paraphrasing each other's statements.

44

Skill Reminder • A **possessive noun** shows ownership or possession. • To form the possessive of most singular nouns, add an apostrophe (') + *s*.

▶ Underline each possessive noun. Identify it as *singular* or *plural*.

1. The sandbags added to the levee's strength. _____

2. In spite of the rescuers' efforts, the levee broke. _____

3. The children's schoolbooks were washed away. _____

▶ Rewrite each sentence, using the possessive form of the noun in parentheses ( ). Identify each possessive noun as *singular* or *plural*.

4. The _____ decision was to build floodwalls. **(citizens)** _____

_____

5. The _____ level kept rising. **(river)** _____

_____

6. The _____ fields lay under 15 feet of water. **(farmer)** _____

_____

7. The _____ arrival helped to speed repair work. **(volunteers)** _____

_____

8. The government processed _____ applications. **(farmers)** _____

_____

 TRY THIS! Make a list of five singular and five plural possessive nouns. Write two sentences using a singular and a plural possessive noun from your list.

Name _____

Skill Reminder • Most plural nouns end in *s* or *es*. Singular nouns ending in a consonant and *y* change *y* to *i* before adding *es*.
• Singular possessive nouns end in '*s*. Plural possessives can end in '*s*, *s'*, or *es'*.

▶ Fold the paper along the dotted line. As each spelling word is read aloud, write it in the blank. Then unfold your paper, and check your work. Practice spelling any words you missed.

1. _____

2. _____

3. _____

4. _____

5. _____

6. _____

7. _____

8. _____

9. _____

10. _____

11. _____

12. _____

13. _____

14. _____

15. _____

16. _____

17. _____

18. _____

19. _____

20. _____

SPELLING WORDS

1. children's
2. class's
3. classes'
4. country's
5. countries'
6. sky's
7. skies
8. sun's
9. safety's
10. storms
11. city's
12. cities
13. goose's
14. oxen's
15. people's
16. strangers'
17. geese's
18. armies'
19. allergies
20. mosquitoes

Practice Book
Timeless Treasures

▶ **Read the ad below. Use context clues to determine the meanings
of the Vocabulary Words. Then write each Vocabulary Word in
the group where it belongs.**

**Be <u>sociable</u>! Join your friends and neighbors at a
demonstration of our newest product!
We call it THE PLOW!**

We've been <u>scouring</u> our Stone Age world to bring you every kind of up-to-the-
minute, <u>newfangled</u> invention to make your life easier. Here's our latest one, fresh
from the rich lands where the Sumerians have <u>flourished</u> for years. Use THE PLOW,
and you'll be <u>astounded</u> when you see how easily you can break up the soil to get it
ready for planting. You, too, can now have a <u>reliable</u> source of grain year after year.
Just grow your own!

Cooking tools are another <u>specialty</u> at SCRATCH 'N PLANT TOOLS.
Remember to buy some of our handy sharp sticks to <u>skewer</u> your meat before
you roast it.

1. _____ amazed, shocked

2. _____ featured item, unique feature

3. _____ pierce, puncture

4. _____ pleasant, friendly

5. _____ modern, up-to-date

6. _____ thrived, succeeded

7. _____ dependable, responsible

8. _____ searching, combing

9. Which Vocabulary Word tells how people from the Stone Age would probably

   feel if they saw airplanes and computers? _____

10. Which Vocabulary Word describes people who enjoy being in groups?

    _____

Write a newspaper ad for a product that would amaze people from the Stone Age.
Use at least three of the Vocabulary Words.

Name _____

HOMEWORK

The Stone
Age News

Main Idea
and Details
TEST PREP

▶ **Read the paragraph. Circle the letter of the best answer to each question.**

After eating an animal's meat, Stone Age people would scrape its skin clean and drape it over their shoulders for warmth. After a fairly short time, though, the skin would rot. Over time, people learned how to preserve hides and make leather from them. They stretched out the skins and set them to dry in the sun. Drying made the hides stiff and hard, but they lasted much longer. People rubbed oil and fat into the skins to soften them. Some people even chewed on hides to make them more flexible. Later, people discovered a natural substance, tannic acid—or *tannin*—that was a great preservative of leather.

1 What is the main idea of this paragraph?

 A Stone Age people wore skins for warmth.

 B People learned how to make leather.

 C Skins rotted after a short time.

 D Tannin preserves leather.

💡 **Tip**

Remember, the main idea is not always found in the first sentence of a paragraph. Find the sentence that most of the other sentences in the paragraph tell more about.

2 Which sentence(s) best support the main idea of the paragraph?

 F sentences 1–3

 G sentence 3 only

 H sentences 4–8

 J sentence 8 only

💡 **Tip**

Which sentence or sentences give more details that directly relate to the main idea?

3 Which detail would NOT support the paragraph's main idea?

 A Tannin—which can be used for treating animal skins—is found in some trees' bark.

 B Some early people soaked animal skins in ashes.

 C Softened skins were more comfortable.

 D People hunted animals for meat.

💡 **Tip**

Eliminate answers that <u>support</u> the main idea.

© Harcourt

SCHOOL-HOME CONNECTION With your child, examine paragraphs in textbooks and newspapers. Have your child identify main ideas in the paragraphs. Discuss how often these main ideas are clearly stated.

Practice Book
Timeless Treasures

Name _____

▶ **Read the paragraph. Then circle the letter of the best answer to each question.**

Creating art has always been important to human cultures. It was especially important to early people who made the amazing cave paintings, often of animals and the hunt, found in France and Spain. People created these works of art deep inside caves, lighting the blackness with torches or crude candles. With frayed sticks or their fingers, artists applied paint made from natural substances mixed with animal fat or blood. Even though many paints were poisonous, some artists put paint in their mouths and blew it through hollow bones onto cave walls.

1. Which of the following statements is a generalization?

    A Creating art has always been important to human cultures.

    B Artists applied paint made from natural substances.

    C People created these works of art deep inside caves.

2. Reread the last sentence of the paragraph. What generalization can you make based on it?

    F Early painters had no desire to live.

    G Early painters were willing to take risks to make art.

    H Early painters were foolish and untalented.

3. Which fact does <u>not</u> support the generalization: *Hunting was extremely important to early people.*

    A Many of the cave paintings showed animals that people hunted.

    B Early people had religious rituals connected with hunting.

    C Early people sometimes painted geometric figures and dots.

▶ **Read each sentence. Write a generalization that you could make based on it.**

4. Thousands of people have visited sites of early cave paintings.

_____

5. There are cave paintings in Europe, and many exist in North America as well.

_____

6. Some cave paintings of hunts are expertly done and show a lot of emotion.

_____

SCHOOL-HOME CONNECTION Read a newspaper article with your child. Work together to come up with one valid and one invalid generalization based on the facts in the article.

49

© Harcourt

Name _____

The Stone
Age News

Grammar:
Subject and
Object Pronouns

Skill Reminder • A **pronoun** takes the place of one or more nouns. • A pronoun's **antecedent** is the noun or nouns to which the pronoun refers. A pronoun must agree with its antecedent in number and gender. • **Subject** pronouns (*I, he, she, it, we, they*) replace the subject of a sentence. **Object** pronouns (*me, you, him, her, it, us, them*) replace objects in a sentence.

▶ Underline each pronoun, and circle its antecedent. Write whether it is a *subject* or an *object* pronoun; *singular* or *plural*; and *masculine, feminine,* or *neuter.*

1. Because the basket was woven so tightly, rain could not get through it.

_____

2. The woman had a lot of grain to carry, so she used a basket.

_____

▶ Fill in the blanks with the correct subject or object pronouns.

Miko is a potter. She rolls clay into long, sausagelike shapes. **(3)** _____ are

called coils, and **(4)** _____ builds up the walls of the pots with **(5)** _____.

Miko's brother Shozo is a cook, and **(6)** _____ gave **(7)** _____ one of

her pots. **(8)** _____ says **(9)** _____ is his most prized possession.

 TRY THIS! Write two sentences. Then replace the subjects and objects with subject and object pronouns.

© Harcourt

Name _____

Skill Reminder Many two-syllable words follow the VCCV
pattern. In these words, the first syllable usually has a short
vowel sound.

▶ Fold the paper along the dotted line. As each spelling word is read aloud, write it
in the blank. Then unfold your paper, and check your work. Practice spelling any
words you missed.

1. _____
2. _____
3. _____
4. _____
5. _____
6. _____
7. _____
8. _____
9. _____
10. _____
11. _____
12. _____
13. _____
14. _____
15. _____
16. _____
17. _____
18. _____
19. _____
20. _____

SPELLING WORDS

1. impact
2. scatter
3. pillow
4. velvet
5. import
6. wander
7. baggage
8. parcel
9. witness
10. garlic
11. splendid
12. survive
13. mammal
14. commands
15. transit
16. barley
17. minnow
18. mellow
19. halter
20. plastic

Practice Book
Timeless Treasures

Name _____

▶ **Read the Vocabulary Words. Then complete the fact sheet about China by filling in each blank with a Vocabulary Word.**

terraces	administrative	elaborate
inhabitants	civilization	famine

POPULATION

China is a huge country with more than 1,200,000,000

(1) _____ .

BEGINNINGS

The ancient Chinese **(2)** _____
grew up around the Yellow River, where the land was fertile. As centuries passed,

emperors used an **(3)** _____ system to help them govern
their lands.

GROWING FOOD

Only about 13 percent of China's land is suitable for farming. However, Chinese

farmers make good use of it by cutting **(4)** _____ into the
sides of hills so that they have more land to grow crops. This makes food more plentiful

and reduces the chance of a severe **(5)** _____ .

THEATER

Traditional Chinese theater features costumes that

are colorful and **(6)** _____ .

▶ **Write the Vocabulary Word that fits best in each word group.**

7. hunger, starvation, _____

8. residents, population, _____

9. costly, showy, _____

10. farms, hillsides, _____

TRY THIS! Think of a time in history or an ancient culture that interests you. Write a paragraph about that period or culture. Use at least two Vocabulary Words in your sentences.

Name _____

▶ **Read the paragraph, and look at the maps. Then circle the letter of the best answer to each question.**

The world's largest nation, Russia, had an area of 6,592,800 square miles in 1999. Though far smaller than Russia, both China and the U.S. are larger than most other nations. (Only Canada is larger than these two.) In 1999 China had an area of 3,691,521 square miles, while the U.S. had an area of 3,536,341 square miles.

1 What information can you learn from the maps ONLY?

> 💡 **Tip**
> Find an answer choice that the paragraph does not discuss.

  A the shapes of the three countries

  B that Russia is the largest country

  C that the U.S. is smaller than China

  D that Canada is larger than the U.S.

2 What does the paragraph tell you that the map does not?

> 💡 **Tip**
> Do the maps show any exact numbers?

  F the three countries' population

  G the three countries' exact area

  H that Canada is larger than Russia

  J that China is smaller than the U.S.

3 If the countries' areas were represented on a bar graph, which bar would be shortest?

> 💡 **Tip**
> Remember that in a bar graph the largest item will have the longest bar.

  A Canada's

  B the United States'

  C Russia's

  D China's

© Harcourt

🚐 **SCHOOL-HOME CONNECTION** Read the paragraph at the top of the page with your child. Have your child use the figures in the paragraph to make a bar graph.

53

Practice Book
Timeless Treasures

Name _____

▶ **Think about the information you would find in the reference sources shown below. Then read each sentence, and write the name of the source you should use.**

1. If you were writing a report on China, you would probably begin by reading the "China" article in this reference source. _____

2. This source contains mainly maps, of China as well as other nations.

   _____

3. A list of magazine articles about Chinese art appears in this reference source.

   _____

4. To read news stories on current events in China, you might check the International News section of this reference source. _____

5. To find lists of current statistics such as populations of Chinese cities, you can check this reference source. _____

6. The *Readers' Guide to Periodical Literature* would help you find an article on Chinese education in one of these publications. _____

7. If you want to watch a TV program about China, this source will tell you whether the show is on tonight. It will also tell you the time and channel.

   _____

8. Suppose you want to find out how well Chinese athletes did in the last Olympic Games. This source will give you the statistics you are looking for.

   _____

9. You want to find an article on Chinese pottery that has lots of color photographs. One of these publications would print an article like that.

   _____

10. This weekend you plan to take a break from writing your report. This source will tell you if you'll have good weather for playing soccer in the park.

   _____

SCHOOL-HOME CONNECTION With your child, study the different sections of a daily newspaper. Have your child list information that appears in the newspaper but would *not* appear in magazines, such as a weather forecast.

Practice Book
Timeless Treasures

© Harcourt

Skill Reminder • **A possessive pronoun** shows ownership or possession. It takes the place of a possessive noun. • Be careful not to confuse the possessive pronouns *its, your,* and *their* with the contractions *it's, you're,* and *they're.*

▶ **Circle the correct choice of each pair in parentheses ( ).**

The city where my aunt Mei-lin lives is small, but **(1) (its, their)** park is large and

beautiful. Mei-lin enjoys **(2) (her, his)** daily walks there. When I visited Aunt Mei-lin

and Uncle Chen last summer, we ate **(3) (their, our)** lunches in the park. The house they

live in is much different from **(4) (theirs, mine).**

▶ **Rewrite each sentence on the lines below, correcting errors in the use of possessive pronouns and contractions.**

5. If your going to the festival, I will go with you. _____

_____

6. Seth's costume looks just like your's. _____

_____

7. The other marchers are putting on they're masks. _____

_____

8. Lian had planned to wear a mask from last year, but its broken. _____

_____

© Harcourt

Name _____

Skill Reminder • **Double consonants can occur within a word or at the end of a word.** • **When they occur within a word, the syllable break usually comes between them.**

▶ Fold the paper along the dotted line. As each spelling word is read aloud, write it in the blank. Then unfold your paper, and check your work. Practice spelling any words you missed.

1. _____

2. _____

3. _____

4. _____

5. _____

6. _____

7. _____

8. _____

9. _____

10. _____

11. _____

12. _____

13. _____

14. _____

15. _____

16. _____

17. _____

18. _____

19. _____

20. _____

SPELLING WORDS

1. necessary
2. sheriff
3. surround
4. mattress
5. pattern
6. cannon
7. compass
8. official
9. embarrass
10. caterpillar
11. oppose
12. difficult
13. assist
14. fulfill
15. procession
16. wheelbarrow
17. toboggan
18. colossal
19. possess
20. forbidden

© Harcourt

Name _____

▶ **Read the Vocabulary Words. Then write the Vocabulary Word that best completes each sentence.**

| isolated | ingenious | passageways | archaeologist | quarries | preserved |

The large sandstone blocks in the famous Egyptian pyramids were moved

over land and water from stone **(1)** _____. The

(2) _____ body of the pharaoh was usually placed at

the end of long, twisting **(3)** _____ to protect it from

tomb robbers. What **(4)** _____ builders the ancient
Egyptians were to figure out such complicated corridors! A pyramid can be a real

challenge to an **(5)** _____. The chamber containing the

pharaoh's body is often **(6)** _____ from other parts of the
pyramid and difficult to locate.

▶ **Write the Vocabulary Word that is a synonym for each word below.**

7. alone

_____

8. maintained

_____

9. clever

_____

10. excavations

_____

11. corridors

_____

12. scientist

_____

TRY THIS! Imagine that you are exploring a pyramid. Write a paragraph telling what you discover. Use all Vocabulary Words.

Practice Book
Timeless Treasures

Name _____

▶ **Read the paragraph. Look at the diagrams. Then circle the letter of the best answer to each question.**

A passageway led from the outside of the pyramid to the pharaoh's tomb. At the end of the passageway were two rooms, a storage room and a room for the tomb itself. As the pyramid rose higher and higher, a ramp was built to lift the heavy stones onto the top layers.

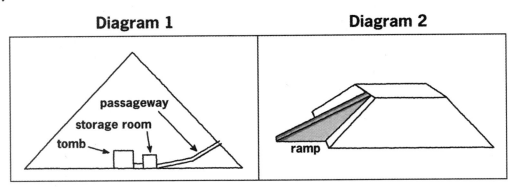

1 Which gives you the best idea of the location of the storage room?

A Diagram 1

B Diagram 2

C the paragraph

 Tip
Eliminate the answer choice that does not deal with the storage room, and decide which of the remaining two gives more specific information.

2 Which does NOT help you understand how the ramp was used?

F Diagram 1

G Diagram 2

H the paragraph

 Tip
Select the answer choice that does not deal with the ramp.

3 If you wanted to find out the exact location of the pyramids, you should

A use a drawing.

B use a map.

C use a time line.

Tip
Think about the kind of source you would use to find out where places or famous landmarks are located.

© Harcourt

SCHOOL-HOME CONNECTION With your child, make a circular diagram based on a clock face. Label and illustrate the key events that occur in a typical school day.

Practice Book
Timeless Treasures

Name _____

| **Skill Reminder** | • **A reflexive pronoun** usually refers to |

the subject of a sentence. It ends with *-self* or *-selves*.
• An **indefinite pronoun** may or may not have a stated
antecedent. Indefinite pronouns are words like *one, some, all, both, everybody,
somebody, anybody, someone, everyone.*

▶ Replace each item in parentheses ( ) with a pronoun, and write it on the line
below. Then write *S* or *O* to tell whether the pronoun is in the subjective or
objective case.

1. **(Men)** built the pyramids of Egypt
   without any cranes or bulldozers.   _____

2. Farmers paid taxes to **(the pharaoh)**
   by helping build the pyramids.   _____

3. The pharaoh would be buried
   inside **(the pyramid).**   _____

4. Petra said, "**(Cairo)** is a
   fascinating city."   _____

▶ Choose an indefinite pronoun to complete each sentence, and write the pronoun
in the blank.

5. _____ of my friends would like to visit the pyramids.

6. _____ knows that they were built thousands of years ago.

7. Anna read a book about Egypt and shared it with _____ of us.

8. _____ on that quiz show won a trip to Egypt.

TRY THIS! Write a conversation between two people. Use all of the indefinite pronouns listed
in the Skill Reminder.

Practice Book
Timeless Treasures

Skill Reminder   In two-syllable words that contain the VCV
spelling pattern, the first syllable may have a long or a short vowel sound.

▶ Fold the paper along the dotted line. As each spelling word is read aloud, write it
in the blank. Then unfold your paper, and check your work. Practice spelling any
words you missed.

1. _____
2. _____
3. _____
4. _____
5. _____
6. _____
7. _____
8. _____
9. _____
10. _____
11. _____
12. _____
13. _____
14. _____
15. _____
16. _____
17. _____
18. _____
19. _____
20. _____

SPELLING WORDS

1. covers
2. granite
3. vital
4. climate
5. novel
6. linen
7. lemon
8. veto
9. limit
10. basis
11. camel
12. silo
13. sequel
14. laser
15. clamor
16. ego
17. panel
18. valid
19. major
20. minute (n.)

© Harcourt

Practice Book
Timeless Treasures

Name _____

▶ **Read the Vocabulary Words and their definitions. Then complete the ancient travel poster by filling in each blank with the best Vocabulary Word.**

emblem: something that stands for something else, such as a nation
mosaic: a design made from bits of colored glass or stone
reconstruct: to put together again
aqueduct: a channel for carrying water from a distance
provinces: parts of a country that are far from the main city
hygiene: practices that keep people clean and healthy

ALL ROADS LEAD TO ROME

On your next trip across the Empire from the outlying **(1)** _____, roam on over to Rome!

Rest from your travels, and improve your personal **(2)** _____ by trying out our warm, comfortable public baths. Buy a plan of the baths so you and your neighbors can **(3)** _____ them in your hometown!

Our city has an up-to-date water supply. Just taste the water carried by our world-famous **(4)** _____.

Museum-quality artworks are our specialty. View the famous statue of our city's founders, which is the **(5)** _____ of Rome.

Expect a fine place to stay. Admire the colorful **(6)** _____ decorations on the wall of the luxury home where your hosts will make you welcome.

▶ **Write the Vocabulary Word that fits best in each word group.**

7. rebuild, remake, _____

8. health, cleanliness, _____

9. pipeline, waterway, _____

10. decoration, design, _____

11. sign, badge, _____

12. territories, states, _____

Practice Book
Timeless Treasures

▶ **Read the paragraph. Then circle the letter of the best answer to each question.**

The old saying, "All roads lead to Rome," is based on the fact that the ancient Romans built a large system of roads. The road system linked Rome with all of its provinces—both nearby and as far away as what is now England. <u>One use of the road system was for military purposes</u>. Soldiers could use the straight paved roads to get to any part of the Roman Empire quickly. The roads also made it easier to transport goods. Roman roads were so well constructed that many are still in use today.

1 What is the main idea of the paragraph?

A Roman roads were straight and paved.

B Some roads linked Rome to England.

C The Romans built a large system of roads.

D Some Roman roads are still in use today.

💡**Tip**
Which answer choice summarizes the paragraph?

2 The underlined sentence is a supporting detail because

F it explains one way the road system was used.

G it compares Roman roads to modern roads.

H it shows that the Romans were often at war.

J it explains why the Romans built so many roads.

💡**Tip**
Look for the relationship between the main idea and the underlined sentence.

3 Which detail would NOT support the main idea?

A One famous Roman road was the Appian Way.

B The oldest Roman roads were built around 300 B.C.

C The Romans built about 50,000 miles of roads.

D The mountains in Greece made it difficult to build roads there.

💡**Tip**
Try using each answer choice as the second sentence of the paragraph. Which choice does not make sense?

SCHOOL-HOME CONNECTION Discuss with your child a past event that you both enjoyed. Have him or her write a paragraph that begins, "We had a good time at _____ because _____." Check that he or she includes details that support this main idea.

Practice Book
Timeless Treasures

© Harcourt

Name _____

Look Into the Past:
The Greeks and
the Romans

Grammar:
Adjectives and
Articles

| **Skill Reminder** | • **Adjectives** modify, or describe, nouns or pronouns. Adjectives tell *what kind, which one,* or *how many.* • The adjectives *a, an,* and *the* are called **articles.** |

▶ **Rewrite the sentences on the lines below. Replace each blank with the type of adjective called for in parentheses ( ).**

1. Greeks sat in _____ amphitheaters to watch plays. **(what kind)**

   _____

2. The _____ performance of a play was in Athens. **(which one)**

   _____

3. Greek plays are still performed in _____ theaters. **(what kind)**

   _____

4. Actors wore masks with only _____ expression. **(how many)**

   _____

5. Actors had to have _____ voices in order to be heard. **(what kind)**

   _____

▶ **Underline the article in parentheses ( ) that correctly completes the sentence.**

6. The Colosseum is (a, an) famous building in Rome.

7. (A, An) emperor of Rome was (a, an) absolute ruler.

8. (A, The) Romans built roads that still exist today.

TRY THIS! Reread the first two pages of "Look Into the Past." Find two examples each of adjectives that tell what kind and how many, and write them down.

Name _____

Look Into the Past:
The Greeks and
the Romans

Spelling: Latin
Roots *-vis-*
and *-dict-*

Skill Reminder　**When prefixes, suffixes, or both are added to the Latin roots *-vis-* or *-dict-*, the spelling of the root word usually stays the same.**

▶ Fold the paper along the dotted line. As each spelling word is read aloud, write it in the blank. Then unfold your paper, and check your work. Practice spelling any words you missed.

1. _____
2. _____
3. _____
4. _____
5. _____
6. _____
7. _____
8. _____
9. _____
10. _____
11. _____
12. _____
13. _____
14. _____
15. _____
16. _____
17. _____
18. _____
19. _____
20. _____

SPELLING WORDS

1. advise
2. visited
3. supervise
4. visitors
5. visor
6. visualize
7. vision
8. prediction
9. revising
10. visa
11. visual
12. visible
13. diction
14. dictate
15. televise
16. invisible
17. improvise
18. dictionary
19. dictator
20. contradict

Practice Book
Timeless Treasures

Name _____

▶ Read the Vocabulary Words and their meanings. Then use the Vocabulary Words to complete the webs.

brutes: rough or savage people

virtues: good qualities

rouse: to wake up

democratic: treating everyone the same way

disguised: changed in appearance so as to look like someone or something else or not to be recognized

bellowing: loud crying or roaring

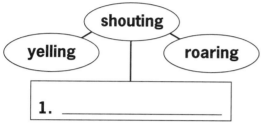

1. _____

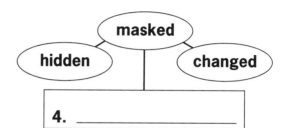

4. _____

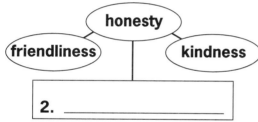

2. _____

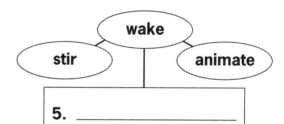

5. _____

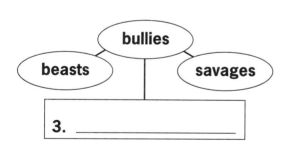

3. _____

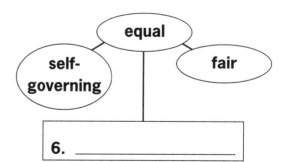

6. _____

▶ Write the Vocabulary Word that means the opposite of each phrase below.

7. speaking softly _____

9. bad qualities _____

8. gentle people _____

10. put to sleep _____

TRY THIS! Write a paragraph about Pericles. Use at least three Vocabulary Words.

Practice Book
Timeless Treasures

© Harcourt

Name _____

▶ **Read the paragraph. Circle the letter of the best answer to each question.**

   The ancient Greek tragedies were major attractions during spring and winter festivals. The earliest tragedies were probably recited by choruses. Later, characters who spoke dialogue interrupted the stories to perform their parts. In many of the plays, the heroes would act so proud, they'd challenge the gods. This tells us something about the psychology of the ancient Greeks. They must have believed that too much pride was dangerous. Greek tragedies are still seen today. It is incredible that these plays are still performed thousands of years after they were written.

1 What is the root of the word *interrupted*? ——

 Tip

Remove the prefix and the suffix from the word *interrupted*.

  A in

  B inter

  C rupt

  D upts

2 Choose the best meaning of the word —— *psychology*.

 Tip

Recall the meaning of *-ology*, and combine it with the meaning of *psych-*.

  F the study of mental processes

  G the study of science

  H something people like to study

  J studying drama or acting

3 Which is the best definition of the word —— *incredible*?

 Tip

The root *-cred* means "believe."

  A not trustworthy

  B hard to believe

  C easy to believe

  D not proved

© Harcourt

 SCHOOL-HOME CONNECTION With your child, create a list of words that end in *-ology*. Talk about the possible meanings of the words.

Practice Book
Timeless Treasures

Name _____

The Skill of
Pericles

Grammar: Proper
and Demonstrative
Adjectives

Skill Reminder • **A proper adjective** is formed from a proper
noun. Many proper adjectives describe nationality or location.
• **A demonstrative adjective** points out a noun and tells *which
one*. The words *this, that, these,* and *those* are demonstrative adjectives.

▶ Write the proper adjective that replaces the words in
parentheses ( ).

1. The greatest _____ statesman was Pericles.
   (of Athens)

2. He was also a great _____ general. **(of Greece)**

3. In some battles he fought _____ soldiers.
   (from Egypt)

4. At home, he battled _____ troops. **(of Sparta)**

5. The fame of Pericles was well known to _____
   leaders. **(of Rome)**

6. His military strategies were familiar to _____
   generals. **(from Europe)**

▶ Rewrite each sentence, using the correct demonstrative adjective in parentheses ( ).

7. (This, Those) statues by Phidias were not made of marble.

_____

8. Look at (that, these) material closely.

_____

9. (This, These) substance is ivory.

_____

10. (This, Those) cloth was made from gold.

_____

TRY THIS! Work in pairs. Look in a dictionary to find ten proper adjectives that you have not
used before. Then use them in sentences of your own.

Practice Book
Timeless Treasures

Skill Reminder   **Many English words include parts that are borrowed from the Greek language.**

▶ Fold the paper along the dotted line. As each spelling word is read aloud, write it in the blank. Then unfold your paper, and check your work. Practice spelling any words you missed.

1. _____

2. _____

3. _____

4. _____

5. _____

6. _____

7. _____

8. _____

9. _____

10. _____

11. _____

12. _____

13. _____

14. _____

15. _____

16. _____

17. _____

18. _____

19. _____

20. _____

SPELLING WORDS

1. physician
2. physical
3. economy
4. politician
5. democracy
6. athlete
7. astronomy
8. microscope
9. hexagon
10. biography
11. biology
12. telephone
13. graphics
14. synthetic
15. symphony
16. toxic
17. atmosphere
18. photography
19. geography
20. thermos

© Harcourt

Name _____

▶ **Complete Sam's letter by filling in each blank with a Vocabulary Word.**

foundation	discouraging	nourishing	migration
remote	edible	cavity	

Dear Eleanor,

I'm not sure when you will get this letter. I am in a very **(1)** _____ location with no mailbox nearby. Just above where I am sitting is a

(2) _____ in a tree. It was hollowed out for a bird's nest. By now

most birds have left on their **(3)** _____ to warmer areas.

The nature book you and I found in the **(4)** _____ of the

old house has been surprisingly helpful. The sections about which plants are

(5) _____ have been really important, but it is

(6) _____ that there seem to be so few of them near where

I'm staying. I wish I'd brought some **(7)** _____ food from home.

Your cousin,
Sam

▶ **Write the Vocabulary Word that fits best in each word group.**

8. base, support, _____

9. distant, isolated, _____

10. hole, hollow, _____

11. nutritious, healthful, _____

12. movement, journey, _____

TRY THIS! Imagine you are interviewing someone who just returned from a month's stay in the mountains. Write five questions to ask in the interview. Use at least three Vocabulary Words in your questions.

Practice Book
Timeless Treasures

Name _____

▶ **Read the paragraph. Circle the letter of the best answer to each question.**

It sounded like a great deal! When the woman at the outdoor store said I could have a free sleeping bag, I leapt at the chance. All I had to do was test the bag and report on how it worked. What a disaster it turned out to be! The bag was as heavy as a load of rocks. I was nearly dead when we finally made camp. Then I didn't get any sleep all night long because the bag was a hot oven. I began to think that the sleeping bag hated me.

1 You know that this paragraph is written from the first-person point of view because

💡 **Tip**
In the first-person point of view, the narrator is a character in the story.

   A the paragraph tells about the first person to try the new sleeping bag.

   B the pronouns *I* and *me* are used.

   C many pronouns are used.

   D there are two characters.

2 What figure of speech is the phrase *the bag was a hot oven*?

💡 **Tip**
First, eliminate answer choices that do not compare things.

   F simile

   G metaphor

   H setting

   J first-person narrator

3 Which is an example of a simile?

💡 **Tip**
Look for the words that signal a simile.

   A The bag was as heavy as a load of rocks.

   B I was nearly dead.

   C I leapt at the chance.

   D The sleeping bag hated me.

© Harcourt

SCHOOL-HOME CONNECTION Ask your child to pretend that a familiar machine, such as a car or a computer, is alive. Help your child write a story that describes the machine's personality. Use a simile or a metaphor in the story.

Practice Book
Timeless Treasures

Name _____

▶ **Choose the best sense word for each description. Write your answer on the line.**

sight	hearing	touch	taste	smell

1. Sam ate the old, dried apple even though it was like chewing sawdust. _____

2. Warblers filled every branch of the huge tree. _____

3. The rotting apples had a strong, bitter odor that appealed to the geese. _____

4. One soft, velvety baby goose brushed up against him. _____

5. The geese took off in a thunderous explosion. _____

▶ **Find three words in the list below to describe each sense. Write them on the lines. Then add two of your own words to each category.**

fishy	peep	jingle	damp	buzz
silky	furry	salty	tangy	

6. hearing _____

7. touch _____

8. taste _____

▶ **Write an image to describe each of the following.**

9. The way the trees smell after it rains

_____

10. The way the sky looks during a lightning storm

_____

SCHOOL-HOME CONNECTION Have your child pick something in the kitchen and describe it in three different ways. Each description should tell how the object appeals to one of the senses.

Practice Book
Timeless Treasures

© Harcourt

Skill Reminder • Use the **comparative** form to compare one thing with one other thing. Use the **superlative** form to compare one thing with two or more other things. • For most one-syllable adjectives, add *-er* and *-est* to make comparisons. Use *more, most, less,* and *least* before most adjectives of two or more syllables. Some adjectives have special forms for comparing.

▶ Circle the better choice of the two words in parentheses ( ).

1. The sun was (**warmer, warmest**) at noon than it had been earlier.

2. The fish were (**more plentiful, plentifulest**) in the evening than in the morning.

3. The tree limb was actually (**more long, longer**) than it appeared to be.

4. The boy looked for the (**taller, tallest**) cattails he could find.

5. The (**more big, biggest**) trees in the forest were the hemlocks.

6. Cold spring water is the (**most refreshing, refreshingest**) drink of all.

▶ Rewrite each sentence, replacing the blank with the correct form of the adjective in parentheses ( ).

7. This is the _____ fish I have ever eaten. (**good**) _____

_____

8. I ate _____ food than I usually do. (**much**) _____

_____

9. I felt _____ (**well**) than I expected to. _____

_____

10. I looked _____ than I felt. (**bad**) _____

_____

 TRY THIS! Use several different comparative or superlative adjectives to compare today's weather with that of other days.

Practice Book
Timeless Treasures

© Harcourt

Name _____

Skill Reminder   In a two-syllable word, the location of the syllable break is determined by the word's spelling pattern.

▶ Fold the paper along the dotted line. As each spelling word is read aloud, write it in the blank. Then unfold your paper, and check your work. Practice spelling any words you missed.

1. _____
2. _____
3. _____
4. _____
5. _____
6. _____
7. _____
8. _____
9. _____
10. _____
11. _____
12. _____
13. _____
14. _____
15. _____
16. _____
17. _____
18. _____
19. _____
20. _____

SPELLING WORDS

1. noticed
2. humans
3. balance
4. hammock
5. arrow
6. victor
7. insects
8. hatchet
9. pumpkin
10. checklist
11. liar
12. chaos
13. famous
14. stomach
15. figure
16. client
17. hinder
18. puncture
19. taxi
20. pliers

© Harcourt

Practice Book
Timeless Treasures

Name _____

| presentation | melodious | flawless |
| lilting | legacy | persevered |

▶ **Complete Mrs. Lee's e-mail message to her grandson, using the Vocabulary Words.**

Subject: Last week's entertainment
From: leejm@gomail.com
To: leewt@gomail.com

Last week's entertainment was the best **(1)** _____ we've ever had here at Evergreen. Four talented young ladies gave an absolutely

(2) _____ performance of music, dance, and drama, making

no mistakes at all. One played a lively, **(3)** _____ tune on the piano. Another girl played the violin. One girl gave a speech in the most

(4) _____ voice! Another presented an amazing dance,

carrying on the **(5)** _____ of African dancers from the past.

All four girls have clearly **(6)** _____ in spite of having to practice for long hours. They are truly inspiring!

I'm looking forward to your visit next Saturday.

▶ **Write the Vocabulary Word that means the opposite of the underlined words.**

7. Some students <u>gave up</u>, but others _____.

8. A few students <u>made errors</u>, but most presentations were _____.

TRY THIS! Imagine you are introducing a friend who is going to recite a poem or sing a song. Write the introduction. Use as many of the Vocabulary Words as you can.

Practice Book
Timeless Treasures

© Harcourt

▶ **Read the paragraph. Then circle the letter of the best answer to each question.**

Many kinds of performers must audition before they can use their talents. An actor might have to read part of a play. Dancers may have only a few steps in which to prove they are qualified for a complicated routine. Musicians sometimes compete in contests before they join an orchestra or other musical group. In a blind audition, musicians perform behind a screen so that they are judged only on their ability and not on their demeanor. An important audition can be a test of a performer's determination and tenacity as well as his or her talent.

1 In this paragraph, the word *steps* means

  A stones used to make a path.

  B a series of actions to meet a goal.

  C ledges that are part of a staircase.

  D movements of the feet.

💡**Tip**
Choose the meaning of *steps* that makes the most sense in the context of the paragraph.

2 The word *demeanor* means

  F musical ability.

  G appearance.

  H unkindness.

  J the skill a person has.

💡**Tip**
Reread the sentence in which *demeanor* appears. In this context, which answer choice seems closest in meaning to *demeanor*?

3 The word *tenacity* means

  A a piece of music used for performing.

  B shyness.

  C stubbornness or persistence.

  D confusion.

💡**Tip**
Notice that in the paragraph *tenacity* is paired with *determination*.

© Harcourt

SCHOOL-HOME CONNECTION With your child, use a dictionary to find two or more different meanings for the word *play*. Then ask your child to read the second sentence in the paragraph. What does *play* mean in this sentence?

Practice Book
Timeless Treasures

Skill Reminder • The **main verb** in a verb phrase can have more than one **helping verb.** Sometimes other words, such as *not,* appear between a helping verb and a main verb. • The form of a verb, or the helping verb in a verb phrase, changes to agree in number with the subject of the sentence. This is called **subject-verb agreement.**

▶ **List the verb phrases. Some are interrupted by other words.**

1. The four friends would be performing together. _____

2. Did Jessie want to play Harriet Tubman? _____

3. Maria had been practicing three hours a day. _____

4. Julie might be happy with even a short solo. _____

5. They did not like the results of the auditions. _____

▶ **Rewrite each sentence, using one of the verbs in parentheses ( ). The verb should agree with the subject of the sentence.**

6. At first they **(doesn't, don't)** wear costumes for their show. _____

_____

7. A teacher **(has, have)** taught them to think like professional performers. _____

_____

8. It **(is, are)** their best show ever. _____

_____

9. **(Is, are)** the senior citizens entertained by the girls' show? _____

_____

10. **(Has, Have)** they forgotten about being depressed? _____

_____

TRY THIS! Think of a friend who has musical talent. Write three sentences about your friend. Use a main verb and a helping verb in each sentence.

© Harcourt

Name _____

Skill Reminder • The suffixes -*ance* and -*ence* mean "quality of" or "state of." • A related word often has the same vowel, such as *instant/instance*.

▶ Fold the paper along the dotted line. As each spelling word is read aloud, write it in the blank. Then unfold your paper, and check your work. Practice spelling any words you missed.

1. _____
2. _____
3. _____
4. _____
5. _____
6. _____
7. _____
8. _____
9. _____
10. _____
11. _____
12. _____
13. _____
14. _____
15. _____
16. _____
17. _____
18. _____
19. _____
20. _____

SPELLING WORDS

1. brilliance
2. difference
3. influence
4. ambulance
5. conference
6. allowance
7. reference
8. entrance
9. importance
10. independence
11. instance
12. performance
13. ignorance
14. acceptance
15. elegance
16. abundance
17. attendance
18. intelligence
19. presence
20. evidence

Practice Book
Timeless Treasures

▶ **Use the Vocabulary Words to complete the paragraph.**

persistence	ingenuity	visibility	initial
acknowledged	milestone	inquiries	

Martha Coston invented the signal flares that were used by shipwrecked sailors in the American Civil War. Her life-saving invention made Mrs. Coston

an **(1)** _____ hero. Her husband had the

(2) _____ idea for signal flares, but Martha used the idea and developed it. The idea was that the flares could be used in all kinds of weather and

(3) _____. After years of working with a team of scientists,

Mrs. Coston's **(4)** _____ was rewarded. Her red, white, and

green flares prompted many **(5)** _____ from ship owners. The U.S. Navy, merchant marines, and ocean liner companies all over the world bought

her invention. It was Mrs. Coston's cleverness and **(6)** _____

that led to the development of this **(7)** _____ in naval safety.

▶ **Next to each definition, write the Vocabulary Word and its root word.**

Definition	Vocabulary Word	Root Word
8. requests for information		
9. condition of seeing clearly		
10. refusal to stop		

TRY THIS! What would you like to accomplish? Write three goals for yourself, using at least three Vocabulary Words.

Practice Book
Timeless Treasures

Name _____

▶ **Read the paragraph. Then circle the letter of the best answer to each question.**

When Grace Hopper began programming computers, paper punch cards were used. Unhappy with this method, Grace created a computer code language. However, both early systems of programming left her dissatisfied. She was sure that if computers could be programmed in English, more people could use them. In 1956 she taught a computer to recognize English statements. A few years later, she invented COBOL, the first user-friendly language for computers. Grace's work helped make today's computers accessible to everyone.

1 What is compared and contrasted in this passage?

  A early computer programming and today's computer programming

  B paper punch cards and Grace Hopper

  C computer codes

  D COBOL and the first user-friendly software language

> **Tip**
> To compare and contrast, there must be two objects or ideas that relate to each other.

2 Which word or phrase points out similarities?

  F a few years later

  G if

  H both

  J unhappy

> **Tip**
> Look back in the passage to find the word that leads to two things that are said to be alike.

3 How is the information in this passage organized?

  A Only likenesses are stated.

  B Only differences are stated.

  C The information begins in the present time and moves to the past.

  D The old methods are described first and then compared with new methods.

> **Tip**
> Look at the beginning, middle, and end of the passage. What pattern do you observe?

© Harcourt

SCHOOL-HOME CONNECTION With your child, choose two interesting objects. List several ways in which the objects are alike and several ways in which they are different.

79

Practice Book
Timeless Treasures

Name _____

bandwagon: the idea that you should do something
because everyone else is doing it

loaded words: words that convey a powerful message

testimonial: advice from well-known people to convince
you to think as they do

glittering generalities: sweeping generalizations that may
have little truth

▶ **Read the paragraphs. Underline a word or phrase in the paragraph that signals a persuasive technique. Then write the type of persuasive technique.**

1. What we need are intelligent car owners who do not drive in bad weather, not some useless gizmo that will clean rain and snow off a windshield.

   persuasive technique: _____

2. Everyone in town is using Madam Walker's hair-care products. Why aren't you?

   persuasive technique: _____

3. When it's company slide-show time, I use the Glo-sheet to take notes in the dark. It helps me stay on top of the facts. After just six months of using the Glo-sheet, I've been promoted to vice-president!

   persuasive technique: _____

4. This no-spill bowl is the BEST!! It's so TERRIFIC! You should NEVER serve breakfast without it!

   persuasive technique: _____

5. You know me. I'm an important movie star. I've starred in all your favorite movies. I want to share with you my secret for looking cool. I only use flat-bottomed paper bags for my groceries. The groceries don't fall out, so I don't look clumsy. Be like me. Be cool. Use paper.

   persuasive technique: _____

© Harcourt

SCHOOL-HOME CONNECTION Ask your child
to identify persuasive words in billboard and
newspaper ads and in TV commercials.

80

Practice Book
Timeless Treasures

Name _____

Skill Reminder • An **action verb** tells what the subject does, did, or will do. • A **direct object** tells who or what is affected by the action. An **indirect object** tells to whom or for whom the action is done. • A **transitive verb** is an action verb that has a direct object. An **intransitive verb** is any verb that does not have a direct object.

▶ Complete each sentence, filling in the blank with a direct object. Underline direct objects in the sentences once. Underline any indirect objects in the sentences twice.

1. The Columbia Paper Bag company made _____.

_____

_____

2. A machine gave Margaret E. Knight an _____.

_____

_____

3. Margaret invented a _____.

_____

_____

4. For her work, Margaret was awarded a _____.

_____

_____

▶ Circle the verb in each sentence. Write whether the verb is transitive or intransitive.

5. Ten-year-old Becky invented the Glo-Sheet. _____

6. She showed her parents the painted board. _____

7. Professionals needed her invention. _____

8. Becky's business blossomed . _____

Practice Book
Timeless Treasures

Name _____

Skill Reminder
- **The suffix *-ion* means "action" or "process."**
- **The suffix *-ness* means "the state or quality of" or "condition."**
- **If necessary, be sure to make spelling changes before adding these suffixes.**

▶ Fold the paper along the dotted line. As each spelling word is read aloud, write it in the blank. Then unfold your paper, and check your work. Practice spelling any words you missed.

1. _____
2. _____
3. _____
4. _____
5. _____
6. _____
7. _____
8. _____
9. _____
10. _____
11. _____
12. _____
13. _____
14. _____
15. _____
16. _____
17. _____
18. _____
19. _____
20. _____

SPELLING WORDS

1. demonstration
2. dampness
3. freshness
4. meditation
5. lateness
6. education
7. consideration
8. suggestion
9. smallness
10. relation
11. subtraction
12. business
13. inspiration
14. calculation
15. tidiness
16. loneliness
17. silliness
18. newness
19. election
20. creation

© Harcourt

Practice Book
Timeless Treasures

Name _____

▶ Complete the school newspaper article by writing the
Vocabulary Word that best completes each sentence.

| realistic | miniature | three-dimensional |
| dependent | recognition | represent |

Mari Espina Wins Top Prize

Mari Espina was awarded first place in the
Natural Science competition yesterday

in **(1)** _____ of her outstanding
diorama on the food cycle in Biscayne Bay. A diorama is not a flat painting but a

(2) _____ model of a scene. Mari used sand

to **(3)** _____ the sea floor. She included
sea creatures made of dough to show how living things in a food chain

are **(4)** _____ on others. "Mari
even carved scales on her fish to make them look more

(5) _____," said Mrs. Frank, the librarian.

"Her scene is a **(6)** _____
model of part of Biscayne Bay."

▶ Write the Vocabulary Word that means the opposite of each word or phrase below.

7. not true-to-life _____

8. life-size _____

9. self-reliant _____

10. flat _____

TRY THIS! What materials would you use to make a diorama showing life in a rain forest, in
a desert, or on the prairie? Write a paragraph describing how you would create a
diorama of one of these places. Use as many of the Vocabulary Words as you can.

Practice Book
Timeless Treasures

Name _____

▶ **Read the paragraph. Circle the letter of the best answer to each question.**

> In science class, Kevin is studying fish and frogs. He has learned that both fish and frogs are good swimmers. While fish spend all their lives in water, most frogs live part of their lives in water and part on land. Fish propel themselves through water by moving from side to side. Frogs swim with the help of webbed feet. The bodies of fish are covered by scales, but frogs have smooth skin. Fish vary greatly in size, from tiny goby fish to whale sharks that can grow to be fifty feet long. In contrast, most frogs are small animals.

1 What is one way in which fish and frogs are similar?

Tip
Find the sentence that tells about both fish and frogs.

   A Both are good swimmers.

   B Both swim from side to side.

   C Both have scales.

   D Both live only in water.

2 Why is the class studying fish and frogs at the same time?

Tip
First, eliminate answer choices that have inaccurate facts.

   F because they are both animals

   G because they are both animals that live in water

   H because they both have webbed feet

   J because they are the same size

3 How are fish different from frogs?

Tip
If necessary, reread the paragraph to see which answer choice is a difference between fish and frogs.

   A Only fish have scales.

   B Only fish are small animals.

   C Only fish are good swimmers.

   D Only fish have smooth skin.

© Harcourt

SCHOOL-HOME CONNECTION Ask your child to describe two people or two stories that he or she has recently read. Then help your child write three sentences comparing and contrasting the people or stories.

Practice Book
Timeless Treasures

Skill Reminder • **A linking verb** links the subject of a sentence to a word in the predicate that renames or describes the subject. • If this word is a noun or a pronoun, it is called a **predicate nominative.** • If this word is an adjective, it is called a **predicate adjective.**

▶ Circle the linking verb in each sentence. Write the predicate nominative or predicate adjective on the line, and label it. Use the abbreviations *P.A.* and *P.N.*

1. The dioramas were huge successes. _____

2. Many of them looked fancy. _____

3. Mari felt nervous about her work. _____

▶ Rewrite each sentence. Replace the blank with a predicate nominative or predicate adjective, along with any other words needed.

4. Mrs. Frank's idea sounded _____. _____

_____

5. The prizes for honorable mention were _____. _____

_____

6. After Mari won, everyone seemed _____. _____

_____

7. Compared with some others, Mari's diorama looked _____. _____

_____

8. Mari's mother felt _____. _____

_____

TRY THIS! Find sentences in the two first pages of "A Do-It-Yourself Project" with linking verbs and predicate nominatives or predicate adjectives. Write down the ones you find.

Name _____

Skill Reminder • The suffixes *-ment* and *-ity* can be added to words to form nouns. • When *-ity* is added to a word that ends in e, the e is usually dropped.

▶ Fold the paper along the dotted line. As each spelling word is read aloud, write it in the blank. Then unfold your paper, and check your work. Practice spelling any words you missed.

1. _____

2. _____

3. _____

4. _____

5. _____

6. _____

7. _____

8. _____

9. _____

10. _____

11. _____

12. _____

13. _____

14. _____

15. _____

16. _____

17. _____

18. _____

19. _____

20. _____

SPELLING WORDS

1. excitement
2. amazement
3. community
4. government
5. ability
6. activity
7. statement
8. environment
9. majority
10. security
11. apartment
12. improvement
13. judgment
14. electricity
15. identity
16. opportunity
17. authority
18. purity
19. resentment
20. basement

© Harcourt

Practice Book
Timeless Treasures

Name _____

▶ Read the Vocabulary Words. Then use the Vocabulary Words to complete the webs.

portable   ornamental
forge   tributes
rugged   install

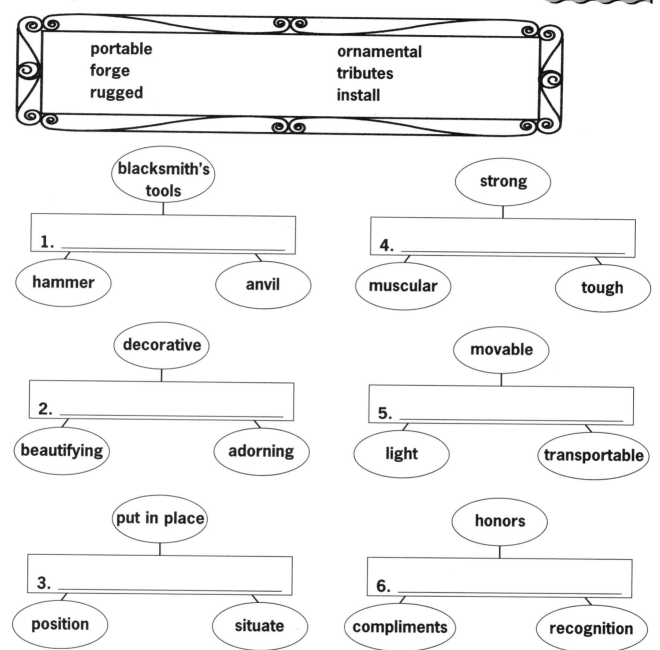

blacksmith's tools

1. _____

hammer   anvil

strong

4. _____

muscular   tough

decorative

2. _____

beautifying   adorning

movable

5. _____

light   transportable

put in place

3. _____

position   situate

honors

6. _____

compliments   recognition

▶ Write the Vocabulary Words that best complete the sentence.

The king's sturdy, **(7)** _____ workers took their light,

(8) _____ tools with them to help them **(9)** _____

some fancy, **(10)** _____ ironwork over the castle doors.

87

Name _____

HOMEWORK

**Catching the Fire:
Philip Simmons,
Blacksmith**

Word Relationships
TEST PREP

▶ **Read the paragraph. Then circle the letter of the best answer to each question.**

Jacqueline's grandfather was a blacksmith who created beautiful iron gates and fences. Although Jacqueline is proud of all of his work, her favorite object is a gate with a dove. It represents freedom from war and is a symbol of peace. Her grandfather also decorated gates with bass and other fish. Jacqueline has many tales of her grandfather's adventures that she likes to share with her friends. Most of all she remembers his deep bass voice and the ring of his hammer when he was at work at his forge.

1 The word *peace* means

   A fragment.

   B agreement or harmony.

   C section or bit.

   D the amount of work done.

💡 **Tip**
Think about the differences between *peace* and its homophone.

2 The word *object* in this paragraph means

   F part of a sentence that follows a verb.

   G goal or purpose.

   H be opposed to or feel dislike for.

   J item that can be seen or touched.

💡 **Tip**
Homographs are words that are spelled alike but have different meanings and pronunciations. Use context to help you figure out which pronunciation and meaning is being used here.

3 In this paragraph, the word *ring* means

   A a holder for keys.

   B a clear sound, like a bell.

   C a thin circle of metal, often made of gold.

   D a place where prizefights take place.

💡 **Tip**
Use context to decide which meaning of *ring* is intended here.

© Harcourt

SCHOOL-HOME CONNECTION Have your child give at least two meanings for each of the following multiple-meaning words: *yard*, *plate*, and *trunk*. Together, write sentences that show the different meanings.

88

Practice Book
Timeless Treasures

Name _____

Catching the Fire:
Philip Simmons,
Blacksmith

Grammar: Simple
Tenses; Present
Tense

Skill Reminder • **Verb tenses** tell the time an action occurs. Verb tenses change to indicate that events happen at different times. • The **simple tenses** are the *present*, the *past*, and the *future*. • The **present tense** shows action that is happening now or that happens over and over.

▶ **Circle the present-tense form of the verb in each sentence.**

1. John Vlach finally **(locates, located)** Philip Simmons in 1972.

2. John **(learned, learns)** much about the South Carolina blacksmith.

3. John **(had, has)** many visits with Philip over four years.

4. Philip **(teaches, taught)** John many things about his work.

5. Vlach's book **(was, is)** about Simmons.

▶ **Rewrite each sentence, using the present-tense form of the verb in parentheses ( ).**

6. Philip _____ the image for each piece. **(vary)** _____

_____

7. Several of Philip's pieces _____ quite famous. **(be)** _____

_____

8. Simmons _____ many awards. **(receive)** _____

_____

9. The awards _____ the nation's best artists. **(honor)** _____

_____

 TRY THIS! Imagine you are a newspaper reporter at the Festival of American Folklife, the summer-long event in Washington, D.C. Write several headlines about what is happening. Use present-tense verbs.

Name _____

Catching the Fire:
Philip Simmons,
Blacksmith

Spelling: Suffixes
-less, -ive,
and -ous

Skill Reminder • The suffixes *-less*, *-ive*, and *-ous* are adjective-forming suffixes. • If the base word ends with e, drop the final e before adding *-ive* or *-ous*. • For some words, add *i* before *-ous*.

▶ Fold the paper along the dotted line. As each spelling word is read aloud, write it in the blank. Then unfold your paper, and check your work. Practice spelling any words you missed.

1. _____
2. _____
3. _____
4. _____
5. _____
6. _____
7. _____
8. _____
9. _____
10. _____
11. _____
12. _____
13. _____
14. _____
15. _____
16. _____
17. _____
18. _____
19. _____
20. _____

SPELLING WORDS

1. hopeless
2. enormous
3. nervous
4. active
5. creative
6. timeless
7. effective
8. positive
9. bottomless
10. fearless
11. negative
12. curious
13. mysterious
14. delicious
15. heartless
16. serious
17. various
18. ageless
19. detective
20. hilarious

Practice Book
Timeless Treasures

Name _____

▶ **Write the Vocabulary Word that best completes each sentence.**

| uncertainly | conviction | sheepishly | propelled |
| scowl | bustled | elective | |

Teresa was a little embarrassed about having a pen pal.

She looked around **(1)** _____, hoping
no one would notice she was writing a letter. Teresa had

the **(2)** _____ that writing to a
French pen pal would help her in her French

(3) _____. Right now her
French wasn't very good, so she wrote her first

sentence a little **(4)** _____. Her

(5) _____ of frustration quickly became a smile as the class bell

rang. She happily joined the other students who **(6)** _____ around

her, letting herself be **(7)** _____ down the hallway by the crowd
pushing to get to class on time.

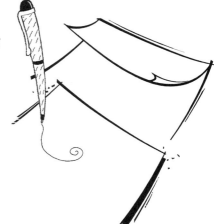

▶ **Write the Vocabulary Word that means the opposite of each word or phrase.**

8. stopped _____

9. disbelief _____

10. required class _____

11. confidently _____

12. trudged slowly _____

13. grin _____

TRY THIS! Find the two verbs and the two adverbs in the list of Vocabulary Words. Put each adverb together with each of the verbs. Which pair works the best? Use that pair in a sentence.

Practice Book
Timeless Treasures

Name _____

▶ **Read the paragraph. Circle the letter of the best answer to each question.**

"Oh sure, I've done lots of ice skating," Jean said with conviction. She had just moved to Maine from Arizona and really wanted to fit in with her new seventh-grade friends. She laced up the rented skates and headed out to the ice-skating area on the frozen pond. "Hold up, skating whiz," laughed her new friend Tonia. "You had better take the skate guards off the blades before amazing us with your talents!" Then Tonia took Jean's arm to help her get started.

1 Based on information in the paragraph, which of these is probably true about Jean?

A She cares what other people think of her.

B She is always truthful.

C She doesn't like ice skating.

D She wants to move back to Arizona.

> **Tip**
> Notice what you learn about Jean in the first few sentences.

2 What evidence in the paragraph supports the conclusion that Tonia is a nice person?

F She calls Jean a "skating whiz."

G She laughs at Jean's inexperience.

H She helps Jean learn to skate.

J She invited Jean to come ice skating.

> **Tip**
> Consider which of these things Tonia really did.

3 Which of these is a valid conclusion that you can draw about Jean?

A She has won ice-skating contests.

B She has never ice skated before.

C She just bought a new pair of ice skates.

D She skates better than her friend Tonia.

> **Tip**
> Follow the events that happen in the paragraph. What conclusion do they lead you to?

© Harcourt

SCHOOL-HOME CONNECTION Tell your child one or two conclusions you have recently drawn about him or her. Then have your child figure out what evidence you used to draw your conclusions.

Practice Book
Timeless Treasures

Name _____

▶ **Read the story in the left column of the chart. Then complete the right column.**

What the Character Says or Does	What This Reveals About the Character
1. It was hard for Josh to concentrate on schoolwork during April. All that Josh could think about then was his favorite baseball team, the Lightning Bolts.	
2. Josh embarrassed himself today when Mr. Carpenter asked the term for the bush country of central Australia. Josh shot his hand into the air and called "Outfield!" instead of "outback."	
3. Even Mr. Carpenter, who rarely smiled, laughed at that one.	
4. Now, strolling home from school, Josh saw Diana, the new girl in his English class. He ran to catch up with her.	
5. "Hi, Josh," she said. "I'm having a birthday party this Saturday, and everyone from our class is invited. Can you come?"	
6. Josh opened his mouth to reply, but no sound came out. The Lightning Bolts were playing on Saturday.	

SCHOOL-HOME CONNECTION With your child, choose someone you both know who is always cheerful. Have your child describe several of the person's actions that show this personality trait.

93

Name _____

Skill Reminder • A verb in the **past tense** shows that the action happened in the past. The past-tense form of regular verbs ends with *-ed.* • The **future tense** of a verb shows that the action will happen in the future. Form the future tense by using the helping verb *will* with the main verb.

▶ Supply the missing verb forms.

Present	Past	Future
1. furrow		
2.	blurred	
3.		will review
4. refer		
5.	allotted	

▶ Rewrite each sentence, using the past tense of the verb in parentheses ( ).

6. The students _____ the parts of speech. **(learn)** _____

_____

7. Victor _____ off to his math class. **(scurry)** _____

_____

8. Victor _____ his favorite magazine. **(receive)** _____

_____

9. All of the models _____ very handsome. **(look)** _____

_____

10. Eventually, Victor _____ scowling. **(stop)** _____

_____

 TRY THIS! Write a sentence in the past tense about something that happened at school yesterday. Then write a future-tense sentence to predict something that will happen tomorrow.

94

Practice Book
Timeless Treasures

Name _____

Skill Reminder • There are two ways to add *-ed* or *-ing* to a word that ends with one vowel and one consonant. • If the final syllable is unstressed, just add the ending. • If the final syllable is stressed or the word has only one syllable, double the final consonant before adding *-ed* or *-ing*.

▶ Fold the paper along the dotted line. As each spelling word is read aloud, write it in the blank. Then unfold your paper, and check your work. Practice spelling any words you missed.

1. _____
2. _____
3. _____
4. _____
5. _____
6. _____
7. _____
8. _____
9. _____
10. _____
11. _____
12. _____
13. _____
14. _____
15. _____
16. _____
17. _____
18. _____
19. _____
20. _____

SPELLING WORDS

1. gathering
2. wondered
3. suffering
4. bragged
5. upsetting
6. scrubbing
7. quarreled
8. referring
9. equipped
10. marveled
11. traveling
12. labeled
13. scanning
14. lingered
15. offering
16. widened
17. pleaded
18. repelled
19. snooping
20. pretending

Practice Book
Timeless Treasures

Name _____

▶ **Read the Vocabulary Words. Then write the Vocabulary Word that correctly completes each row in the chart.**

| gestured | muster | significance |
| tentative | appreciatively | mystified |

General Meaning	Specific Meaning	More Specific Meaning
1. made movements		pointed
2. gather	summon	
3. meaning		importance
4. uncertain	hesitating	
5. with understanding	with feeling	
6. puzzled		astonished

▶ **Write the Vocabulary Word that best completes each sentence.**

7. Minh was confused and _____ by the size of the school.

8. He breathed deeply in an effort to _____ his courage.

9. A tall woman _____ with her arm to the door.

10. Minh paused and then took a _____ step into the classroom.

11. He looked _____ at the welcome sign and felt happy.

12. The words on the sign had a special _____ for Minh.

TRY THIS! Use the words in the chart above to write a conversation among three characters. Each character should use words from only one column.

Practice Book
Timeless Treasures

© Harcourt

▶ **Read the passage. Then circle the letter of the best answer to each question.**

In Vietnam people greet each other with a bow, not a handshake. I wanted Hahn, an exchange student from Vietnam, to feel welcome, so I kept reminding myself to bow. As we were introduced, I clenched my hands in my pockets, but Hahn said hello in perfect English and extended his hand toward me. I laughed as my hand shot out of my pocket. It missed Hahn's hand and our arms crossed in a big X. We both laughed as we finally connected in a firm handshake. Then we bowed to each other, and we laughed again.

1 What is the author's main purpose in this passage?

A to give information

B to give directions

C to entertain

D to persuade

Tip
Eliminate the answer choices that are clearly wrong.

2 What is the author's perspective in this passage?

F This was a sad moment.

G This was an amusing moment.

H This was an angry moment.

J This was a serious moment.

Tip
Look at the author's choice of words and images. How do the author's choices make you feel?

3 Which of the following does the author want you to believe?

A The students have known each other for a long time.

B The students are both very uncomfortable.

C The students will not become friends.

D The students will probably become friends.

Tip
Reread how the students react to each other. What can you predict from their behavior?

SCHOOL-HOME CONNECTION With your child, discuss programs on television that inform (news), entertain (comedies), or persuade (ads or commercials).

Practice Book
Timeless Treasures

Name _____

Skill Reminder The four basic forms of a verb are called its **principal parts.** These forms are the *infinitive,* the *present participle,* the *past tense,* and the *past participle.*

▶ Underline each participle, and tell which form it is.

1. The runner is walking with crutches. _____

2. She had injured her leg in the race. _____

3. The crowd is applauding her. _____

▶ Write the present and past participle of each verb.

	Present Participle	**Past Participle**
4. compete	_____	_____
5. race	_____	_____
6. succeed	_____	_____
7. finish	_____	_____

▶ Rewrite each sentence. Use the correct principal part of the verb in parentheses ( ). Then tell which principal part you used.

8. Our team has _____ the stadium. **(enter)** _____

   _____

9. The contestants are _____ their muscles. **(stretch)** _____

   _____

10. They have _____ the crowd with their skill. **(electrify)** _____

   _____

TRY THIS! Write the present participle form of five verbs. Then combine them with helping verbs such as *is* and *were,* and use them in sentences.

Practice Book
Timeless Treasures

© Harcourt

Name _____

Skill Reminder   Before *b, p,* or *m*, this prefix is usually spelled
com-.

▶ Fold the paper along the dotted line. As each spelling word is read aloud, write it
in the blank. Then unfold your paper, and check your work. Practice spelling any
words you missed.

1. _____

2. _____

3. _____

4. _____

5. _____

6. _____

7. _____

8. _____

9. _____

10. _____

11. _____

12. _____

13. _____

14. _____

15. _____

16. _____

17. _____

18. _____

19. _____

20. _____

SPELLING WORDS

1. composition
2. complicated
3. complaint
4. comfortable
5. construction
6. constant
7. conversation
8. comparison
9. combine
10. commander
11. consider
12. condition
13. conviction
14. confidence
15. concern
16. committee
17. commitment
18. context
19. confess
20. companion

Practice Book
Timeless Treasures

Name _____

▶ **Read the Vocabulary Words. Use one Vocabulary Word to complete each web.**

| precision | devised | transcribed |
| gradually | dormitory | stylus |

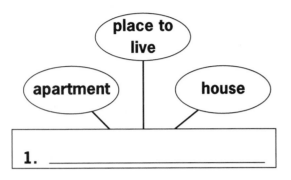

place to live

apartment   house

1. _____

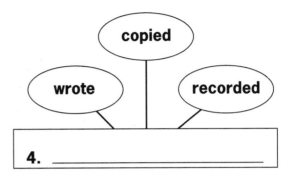

copied

wrote   recorded

4. _____

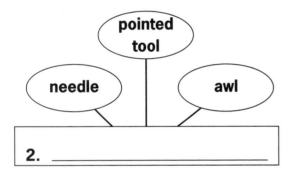

pointed tool

needle   awl

2. _____

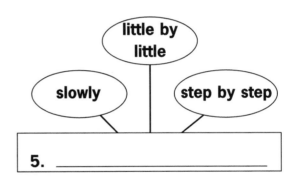

little by little

slowly   step by step

5. _____

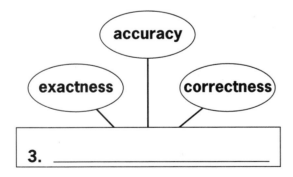

accuracy

exactness   correctness

3. _____

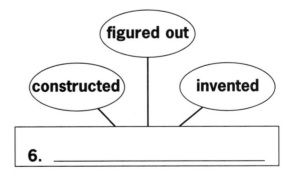

figured out

constructed   invented

6. _____

TRY THIS! Think of an action or task that should be done gradually and with precision. Write two sentences describing the action or task. Use *gradually* and *precision*.

© Harcourt

Name _____

▶ **Read the paragraph. Circle the letter of the best answer to each question.**

Until Louis Braille was ten years old, he lived in a small, pleasant town in the country. Then he went away to school in Paris, where the air was damp and cold. The large school building was confusing to Louis, and there were so many students that he couldn't remember people's names. He missed his family and his country home, and worse, he quickly developed a persistent cough. However, Louis soon got into the routine of going to class. He made friends, and he learned to play the piano. For the rest of his life he would be a great lover of music.

1 Which conclusion can you draw about why Louis developed a cough?

A The school did not have a heating system.

B The damp and cold of Paris affected him.

C He preferred life in his small country hometown.

D It is not healthy to live in big cities.

💡Tip
Eliminate illogical choices. Choose the one from the remaining choices that is written about in the paragraph.

2 What evidence suggests that Louis was unhappy when he first came to the school?

F He was lonesome for his family and his country home.

G He did not like the teachers.

H His family had sent him there.

J The other students didn't like him.

💡Tip
Choose the answer that directly relates to Louis's feelings.

3 What evidence supports the conclusion that Louis eventually became happy at the school?

A He began to fall in love with Paris.

B There were many students at the school.

C He made friends and learned to play the piano.

D He did not want to return to his hometown.

💡Tip
Look for evidence that actually appears in the paragraph.

© Harcourt

SCHOOL-HOME CONNECTION With your child, watch part of a television comedy with the sound off. What conclusions can you draw about what is being said? On what evidence do you base your conclusions?

Practice Book
Timeless Treasures

Name _____

Out of Darkness:
The Story of
Louis Braille

Grammar:
Regular and
Irregular Verbs

Skill Reminder • The past and the past participle of **regular verbs** are formed by adding *-d* or *-ed*. • The past and the past participle of **irregular verbs** are formed in several other ways.

▶ Write the past and past participle of each verb in the blanks provided.

	Past	Past Participle
1. choose	_____	_____
2. lose	_____	_____
3. ring	_____	_____
4. catch	_____	_____
5. wear	_____	_____

▶ Complete the passage with words from the box.

began	grew	frozen	swam	broke

CLAP!
CLAP!

Louis had just **(6)** _____ his fifteenth year at the time of the assembly.

As they watched, the audience members **(7)** _____ quite interested. Possibilities

(8) _____ in Dr. Pignier's mind. What might this lead to? By the end of the

demonstration, the people in the audience had **(9)** _____ in wonder. Then they

(10) _____ into applause.

TRY THIS! Louis Braille used the sense of touch to "see" letters and words. Use past-tense forms of the verbs *touch, feel,* and *rub* to write sentences about three things you did yesterday. Which verb is irregular? How do you know?

Skill Reminder	Adding *under-, in-, trans-, mid-, sub-,* or *pro-* to words usually does not require any spelling changes.

▶ Fold the paper along the dotted line. As each spelling word is read aloud, write it in the blank. Then unfold your paper, and check your work. Practice spelling any words you missed.

1. _____
2. _____
3. _____
4. _____
5. _____
6. _____
7. _____
8. _____
9. _____
10. _____
11. _____
12. _____
13. _____
14. _____
15. _____
16. _____
17. _____
18. _____
19. _____
20. _____

SPELLING WORDS

1. underrated
2. underground
3. submarine
4. transportation
5. understand
6. subscribe
7. inhale
8. transmit
9. transform
10. undertake
11. midway
12. subtitle
13. instructor
14. invest
15. midnight
16. install
17. midair
18. midterm
19. translate
20. submerge

Practice Book
Timeless Treasures

Name _____

▶ Complete the poem by filling in each blank with the best
Vocabulary Word. Hint: Some Vocabulary Words rhyme with
words in the poem.

| dramatically | irresistible | fluster |
| solemnly | sublime | bewildered |

Home-made ice cream is

(1) _____ and

(2) _____ in summertime.
I made some for my friends last night. My best
friend took the first big bite. She asked

(3) _____, loud and
clear, "Whatever did you put in here?" I was

shocked, (4) _____, in a

(5) _____. Instead of
lemon, I put in mustard. In the future I

(6) _____ swear to read
the recipe with more care.

▶ Write the Vocabulary Word that best fits in each word group.

7. seriously, earnestly, gravely, _____

8. expressively, theatrically, emotionally, _____

9. confused, puzzled, uncertain, _____

10. majestic, awesome, magnificent, _____

11. confusion, excitement, agitation, _____

12. overpowering, compelling, forceful, _____

TRY THIS!

Write a word or phrase that means the opposite of each Vocabulary Word.

© Harcourt

Practice Book
Timeless Treasures

▶ **Read the paragraph. Then circle the letter of the best answer to each question.**

Anne of Green Gables is a novel of local color, including many descriptions of locations on Prince Edward Island. The domestic events in Anne's new home, as well as her adventures farther afield, make the reader well-acquainted with the island. Though many years have passed, tourists intending to vacation on Prince Edward Island today will feel quite at home there if they have read the novel.

1 Which is the best definition for *local color*?

  A the changing of leaves in the autumn

  B painting landscapes close to home

  C set on an island

  D filled with details about a setting or region

💡 **Tip**

Reread the first sentence, in which the term *local color* appears. Find the context clue in that sentence.

2 Which is the best definition for *afield*?

  F in the outdoors

  G during picnics

  H away from one's home

  J while walking or hiking

💡 **Tip**

Find *afield* in the second sentence. What is *afield* contrasted with?

3 Which phrase is a context clue that helps you understand that *domestic* means "relating to family or home?"

  A "descriptions of locations"

  B "in Anne's new home"

  C "Prince Edward Island today"

  D "well-acquainted with the island"

💡 **Tip**

Have you figured out what *domestic* in the second sentence means? Which of these phrases helped you?

SCHOOL-HOME CONNECTION Have your child read a newspaper article and note any unfamiliar words. Then help him or her figure out the meanings of the words from the way they are used in the article.

Practice Book
Timeless Treasures

Name _____

Skill Reminder • There are three perfect tenses—**present
perfect, past perfect,** and **future perfect.** To make the
perfect tenses, use the past participle of the main verb and a form of the
helping verb *have.* • The form of *have* shows the tense. Use *has* or *have*
for the present perfect, *had* for the past perfect, and *will have* for the
future perfect.

▶ Complete the chart with the missing tenses of each verb.

Verb	Present Perfect	Past Perfect	Future Perfect
1. look	has, have looked		
2. wear		had worn	
3. bring	has, have brought		
4. grown			will have grown

▶ Rewrite each sentence, replacing the underlined verb
with the tense called for in parentheses ( ).

5. Marilla <u>lost</u> her brooch. **(present perfect)** _____

_____

6. Marilla <u>accuses</u> Anne of losing it. **(present perfect)** _____

_____

7. Anne <u>has</u> never <u>told</u> Marilla a lie before. **(past perfect)** _____

_____

8. By the time she gets to the picnic, <u>will</u> Anne <u>miss</u> the ice cream? **(future perfect)**

_____

_____

TRY THIS! Write a letter Anne might have written to a friend. Use several perfect tense verbs
in the letter.

© Harcourt

Name _____

Skill Reminder The prefixes *dis-* and *non-* mean "not" or "the opposite of."

▶ Fold the paper along the dotted line. As each spelling word is read aloud, write it in the blank. Then unfold your paper, and check your work. Practice spelling any words you missed.

1. _____
2. _____
3. _____
4. _____
5. _____
6. _____
7. _____
8. _____
9. _____
10. _____
11. _____
12. _____
13. _____
14. _____
15. _____
16. _____
17. _____
18. _____
19. _____
20. _____

SPELLING WORDS

1. disrespect
2. disorder
3. nonreturnable
4. nonconformist
5. disgraced
6. nonfiction
7. nonviolent
8. disadvantage
9. disappear
10. disability
11. discomfort
12. disconnect
13. nonresident
14. nonfat
15. disappointed
16. discovery
17. nonpayment
18. nonstandard
19. displeasure
20. distaste

Practice Book
Timeless Treasures

Name _____

▶ Read the Vocabulary Words. Write the Vocabulary Word that best completes each job ad.

full-fledged	ornery	diversion
corralled	compliant	
permeates	craggy	

NOW HIRING to herd cattle on my ranch. Only

(1) _____ cowhands with experience need apply. Call 555-0188.

BEAUTIFUL WORKING CONDITIONS outdoors among rugged, **(2)** _____ hills. Must love horses. Apply in person at 703 Mockingbird Road.

ENJOY BEING OUTDOORS where the scent of wildflowers

(3) _____ the air? Then this job is for you. Call Slim at 555-0148.

TOUGH JOB for tough workers. Some of our cattle are tame and

(4) _____, but others are mean and

(5) _____. If you can keep animals in line in spite

of any **(6)** _____, send your qualifications to P.O. Box 3434.

IF YOU HAVE HERDED CATTLE

and **(7)** _____ horses, you may qualify for a job on our ranch. Call Daisy at 555-0104.

▶ Write the Vocabulary Word with nearly the same meaning as each of these words or phrases.

8. distraction

_____

10. easy-going

_____

12. spreads through

_____

9. completely qualified

_____

11. rough

_____

13. bad-tempered

_____

TRY THIS! Write a paragraph about an ornery horse. Use at least three Vocabulary Words.

Name _____

▶ **Read the paragraph. Circle the letter of the best answer to each question.**

Charles Goodnight, a cattle rancher from Texas, gets credit for inventing the chuck wagon in 1866. Before that time, each cowboy had carried his own food. Goodnight bought an old wagon and outfitted it to serve as a movable kitchen. Cowboys may have eaten more nutritious food at this so-called "chuck wagon" than at modern fast-food restaurants. Many cowboys today eat too much greasy and fried food and not nearly enough fresh fruits and vegetables. Perhaps one day a clever modern rancher will invent a "health wagon" to help modern cowboys improve their diets.

1 What statement expresses the author's perspective about today's cowboys?

A They eat too much.

B They eat the wrong kinds of food.

C They don't eat enough.

D They should carry their own food.

> **Tip**
> Look for details in the passage that lead you to form an opinion of modern cowboys.

2 What evidence supports the author's perspective?

F Charles Goodnight probably served nutritious food from his chuck wagon.

G Today, many cowboys eat fresh vegetables.

H Today, many cowboys eat a lot of greasy and fried food.

J Cowboys have been asking for a "health wagon."

> **Tip**
> Which answer choice supports the author's opinion that you chose in question 1?

3 What is the author's main purpose in this passage?

A to show cause and effect

B to entertain

C to persuade

D to inform

> **Tip**
> First, eliminate answer choices that are clearly wrong.

SCHOOL-HOME CONNECTION With your child, look through magazines or newspapers for examples of persuasive advertisements. Discuss what messages the ads convey.

Practice Book
Timeless Treasures

© Harcourt

Name _____

Skill Reminder • Each verb has **progressive** forms, which tell about action that continues over time. To make the progressive forms, use the present participle of the main verb plus a form of *be* as a helping verb. • Use *am, is,* or *are* for the present progressive; *was* or *were* for the past progressive; and *will be* for the future progressive.

▶ Some of the following sentences contain errors. Rewrite them correctly. Write *correct* next to the sentences without errors.

1. Leedro were riding alone. _____

_____

2. Randy are chasing a yearling. _____

_____

3. Now six cowboys were running after it. _____

_____

4. Soon they will be leading the stray back. _____

_____

5. Last week the cowboys was leading the cattle out. _____

_____

6. Tomorrow they were herding them back to the corrals. _____

_____

▶ Underline the correct form of *be*.

7. The sun (is, are) peeking over the horizon.

8. Earlier, the cowboys (was, were) hurrying to get ready.

9. In an hour, they (is, will be) herding the cattle home.

10. Now the cattle (was, are) heading for the corrals.

TRY THIS! Complete this sentence in three different ways: The cowboys ___?___ working from dawn to dusk. Identify the tense you use in each sentence.

Name _____

Skill Reminder • If the base word begins with *l*, the prefix is spelled *il-*. • If the base word begins with *m*, *p*, or *b*, the prefix is spelled *im-*. • If the base word begins with *r*, the prefix is spelled *ir-*.

▶ Fold the paper along the dotted line. As each spelling word is read aloud, write it in the blank. Then unfold your paper, and check your work. Practice spelling any words you missed.

1. _____
2. _____
3. _____
4. _____
5. _____
6. _____
7. _____
8. _____
9. _____
10. _____
11. _____
12. _____
13. _____
14. _____
15. _____
16. _____
17. _____
18. _____
19. _____
20. _____

SPELLING WORDS

1. impatient
2. impolite
3. irresponsible
4. irregular
5. impossible
6. illegal
7. independent
8. indefinite
9. improper
10. informal
11. immature
12. insecure
13. illegible
14. impure
15. invalid
16. illiterate
17. imbalance
18. inability
19. insane
20. indigestion

Practice Book
Timeless Treasures

Name _____

▶ **Read the Vocabulary Words. Then write the Vocabulary Word that best completes each analogy.**

cylinder	transparent	traditional
submerged	microscopic	collide

1. *Square* is to *cube* as *circle* is to _____.

2. *On* is to *floating* as *under* is to _____.

3. *Puddle* is to *muddy* as *water* is to _____.

4. *Dinosaur* is to *huge* as *germ* is to _____.

5. *Rap music* is to *modern* as *classical music* is to _____.

6. *Silence* is to *talk* as *miss* is to _____.

▶ **Write the Vocabulary Word that best completes each sentence.**

7. If something is so small that you cannot see it, it is _____.

8. If something allows light through it so that you can see to the other side it is

   _____.

9. If something is hidden under water, it is _____.

 TRY THIS! Write the Vocabulary Words that are adjectives. For each word, write at least three nouns that the word could modify.

© Harcourt

Name _____

▶ **Read the paragraph. Then circle the letter of the best answer to each question.**

In the 1500s, a mapmaker named Gerardus Mercator drew a new kind of map. Before this time, early mapmakers had trouble mapping the earth on flat paper. Their maps showed the lines of latitude and longitude as evenly spaced straight lines. These maps ignored the fact that the earth is round, and so they were inaccurate. Early sailors could go off course using them. Mercator's work was so successful that mapmakers today still use the Mercator projection when they make certain kinds of maps.

1 This paragraph begins with

  A a cause

  B an effect

  C a simile

  D a metaphor

💡 Tip

Remember that similes and metaphors are comparisons, a cause is an action, and an effect is a result of an action.

2 Which was NOT a cause of Mercator making a new kind of map?

  F Old maps were ugly.

  G Old maps ignored the fact that the earth is round.

  H Old maps made sailors go off course.

  J Old maps did not show latitude and longitude correctly.

💡 Tip

Reread the paragraph to find the reason that is not mentioned.

3 What is one effect of Mercator's work?

  A He proved that the earth is round.

  B He developed a type of map that is used even today.

  C He showed that latitude and longitude should be drawn as evenly spaced straight lines.

  D He proved that maps made before his were accurate.

💡 Tip

Notice the information given in the final sentence.

© Harcourt

SCHOOL-HOME CONNECTION Watch the news with your child, or read a newspaper with him or her. Discuss cause-and-effect relationships in the news.

Practice Book
Timeless Treasures

Name _____

▶ Before you read the passage below, complete the Question column of the SQ3R chart. Write questions that you expect to find answers to. After you read the passages below, complete the Review column by writing answers to your questions.

Maps: Useful Tools

Kinds of Maps

Not all maps look alike. Their appearance depends on their purpose. For example, a **physical map** shows geographic features of the land, such as mountains, deserts, and bodies of water. A **political map** shows the borders of different countries. A **chart** is a map of water that boaters use; it shows the depth of the sea at different locations.

Map Key

The first place to look to understand a map is the **map key,** or **legend.** A map key explains the symbols and colors used on a map. It also indicates which way is north and the scale of miles.

Survey	Questions	Review
Kinds of Maps	1. _____	6. _____
	2. _____	7. _____
	3. _____	8. _____
	4. _____	9. _____
Map Key	5. _____	10. _____

SCHOOL-HOME CONNECTION Ask your child to tell you about different kinds of maps. If you have a map handy, study the legend together.

114

Practice Book
Timeless Treasures

© Harcourt

Skill Reminder • **A contraction** is the shortened form of two words. An apostrophe takes the place of one or more letters that are left out. • **Negatives** are words whose meaning includes "no" or "not." Negatives include *no, not, never, neither, scarcely,* and *barely.* Use only one negative in a sentence.

▶ **Rewrite each sentence. Replace underlined word groups with contractions.**

1. Flat maps of large areas <u>can not</u> be completely accurate. _____

_____

2. <u>It is</u> not possible to show round surfaces on flat paper. _____

_____

3. <u>You will</u> have to use a globe. _____

_____

4. You <u>will not</u> get an accurate view of the world using an atlas. _____

_____

▶ **Rewrite each sentence, correcting any errors in the use of pronouns, contractions, or negatives.**

5. Hand me you're atlas, please. _____

_____

6. I haven't never looked up Antarctica. _____

_____

7. Don't give me no help finding it. _____

_____

8. I think Ive spotted it. _____

TRY THIS! Reread the first page of "Atlas in the Round." Copy two sentences where contractions could be used. Rewrite the sentences, using the contractions.

Skill Reminder • The prefix *ex-* means "out," "out of," or "beyond." • The prefix *re-* means "back" or "again."

▶ Fold the paper along the dotted line. As each spelling word is read aloud, write it in the blank. Then unfold your paper, and check your work. Practice spelling any words you missed.

1. _____
2. _____
3. _____
4. _____
5. _____
6. _____
7. _____
8. _____
9. _____
10. _____
11. _____
12. _____
13. _____
14. _____
15. _____
16. _____
17. _____
18. _____
19. _____
20. _____

SPELLING WORDS

1. respects
2. exploring
3. restraining
4. recalled
5. released
6. expiration
7. experimented
8. expense
9. regardless
10. reliable
11. repeated
12. exaggerated
13. resolve
14. exceedingly
15. experience
16. extinct
17. export
18. exhibit
19. expression
20. extend

Name _____

▶ **Read the Vocabulary Words. Then write the Vocabulary Word that best completes each sentence.**

| gauge | dissipate | salvage | abounded | diversity | acoustic | buoyancy |

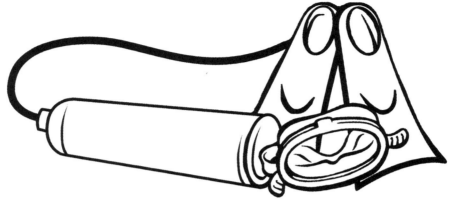

1. Underwater _____ operations allow divers to explore shipwrecks.

2. The oceans have always _____ with many kinds of marine life.

3. There is even greater _____ of life in water than on land.

4. A diver will check the oxygen tank _____ to see how long he or she can stay underwater.

5. Humans need oxygen in their lungs in order to have _____ in water.

6. Air bubbles are created in the water when a diver breathes, but they quickly

_____ .

7. Unlike fish, humans do not have good _____ systems to hear underwater.

▶ **Write the Vocabulary Word that best completes each analogy.**

8. *One* is to *many* as *sameness* is to _____ .

9. *Sight* is to *visual* as *sound* is to _____ .

10. *Gas tank* is to *gas meter* as *oxygen tank* is to _____ .

TRY THIS! Create an advertisement for a sporting goods store that sells scuba-diving equipment. Use as many Vocabulary Words as possible in your description of the items that are for sale.

Practice Book
Timeless Treasures

Name _____

▶ **Read the paragraph. Circle the letter of the best answer to each question.**

Scuba diving is the most exciting of all water sports. The waters off the islands in the Caribbean Sea are the best for underwater exploration. There are hundreds of different species of fish and many kinds of marine life in the deep, clear waters. Some, in fact, haven't even been identified yet by scientists. To explore properly, it is essential to have the proper scuba-diving equipment. A pair of flippers, an oxygen tank, a mask, and a wetsuit are very important. Flippers are the most difficult to get used to. They feel weird, and they make walking extremely difficult!

1 Which of these is a fact about scuba diving?

  A It is the most exciting water sport.

  B Proper equipment is necessary.

  C Flippers feel weird.

  D The Caribbean Sea is beautiful.

> 💡 **Tip**
> Examine the descriptive adjectives in each answer choice.

2 Which of these shows the author's opinion?

  F Many species of fish live in the ocean.

  G One needs equipment to scuba dive.

  H Some species of fish are unknown.

  J Flippers are hard to get used to.

> 💡 **Tip**
> Look for the sentence that is only about the author's beliefs.

3 Which fact does NOT support the author's opinion that the Caribbean is the best place for underwater exploring?

  A Hundreds of kinds of fish swim there.

  B The waters are deep and clear.

  C Good equipment is very important.

  D Many kinds of marine life can be seen in the waters.

> 💡 **Tip**
> Eliminate any answer choice that supports the opinion.

© Harcourt

SCHOOL-HOME CONNECTION Find an interesting newspaper or magazine article. Read the article with your child, and make a list of facts and opinions that you find.

Practice Book
Timeless Treasures

Name _____

▶ **Choose the term with the most positive or most negative meaning, according to the instruction in parentheses ( ). Write the best answer in the blank.**

1. Brian has been _____ all his life. **(positive)**
   a daredevil   **adventurous**   **reckless**

2. He and his brother, Mark, like underwater exploration, even though many people

   consider it _____. **(negative)**
   daring   **adventurous**   **foolhardy**

3. Brian is _____ that he can become a good diver
   with the right equipment. **(positive)**
   overconfident   **uncertain**   **sure**

4. Last week Brian _____ confidently into a
   scuba diving store. **(positive)**
   crept   **walked**   **strode**

5. He tried to pick up an oxygen tank, but he lost his grip, and it

   _____ on the floor. **(negative)**
   thudded   **fell**   **dropped**

6. All of the salesclerks _____ at Brian. **(negative)**
   gazed   **looked**   **glared**

7. "Sorry about that," Brian _____. **(negative)**
   muttered   **stated**   **declared**

8. Brian heard one of the clerks whisper, "He's too _____ to be
   carrying all of that heavy equipment." **(negative)**
   small   **puny**   **little**

9. Fortunately, that experience didn't dim Brian's _____ spirit.
   (positive)
   brash   **bold**   **reckless**

10. Brian believes that being _____ will make it easier for him to
    maneuver in the water. **(positive)**
    scrawny   **skinny**   **slender**

SCHOOL-HOME CONNECTION Read a few
paragraphs from a newspaper story, and underline
several words. Have your child identify each word
as having a positive or negative connotation. Have him or her
think of substitutes for the underlined words. Do they change
the meaning?

Practice Book
Timeless Treasures

Name _____

Skill Reminder • An **adverb** modifies, or describes, a verb, an adjective, or another adverb. Adverbs tell *how, when, where, how often,* or *to what extent.* • **Many adverbs end with -ly.**

▶ **Write the adverb in each sentence and whether it tells *how, when, where, how often,* or *to what extent.***

1. Oxygen tanks allow scuba divers to breathe easily under water. _____

2. A lack of oxygen could be very dangerous. _____

3. Careful divers avoid sudden moves upward. _____

▶ **Underline each adverb. Draw an arrow to the word it modifies. Then write whether that word is a *verb*, an *adjective*, or an *adverb*.**

4. The diver sat anxiously on the deck of the boat. _____

5. She seemed too nervous to dive. _____

6. The waves splashed very gently against her feet. _____

▶ **Rewrite each sentence, completing it with the adverb that makes sense.**

7. Looking at underwater life up close is **(quite, firmly)** exciting to most divers.

_____

_____

8. Many animals attach themselves **(quite, firmly)** to coral reefs for camouflage.

_____

_____

Write a brief paragraph describing an exciting adventure in your life. Use at least one adverb in each of your sentences. After you have completed the paragraph, **THIS!** go back and underline each of the adverbs.

© Harcourt

Name _____

Skill Reminder The prefix *pre-* means "before." The prefix *pro-* means "in front of," "for," or "before."

▶ Fold the paper along the dotted line. As each spelling word is read aloud, write it in the blank. Then unfold your paper, and check your work. Practice spelling any words you missed.

1. _____
2. _____
3. _____
4. _____
5. _____
6. _____
7. _____
8. _____
9. _____
10. _____
11. _____
12. _____
13. _____
14. _____
15. _____
16. _____
17. _____
18. _____
19. _____
20. _____

SPELLING WORDS

1. protected
2. premature
3. preserve
4. provides
5. promotion
6. profile
7. protest
8. proclaim
9. professor
10. pretest
11. preview
12. process
13. prescription
14. proportion
15. propeller
16. precipitation
17. preface
18. prefix
19. preparation
20. pronounce

Practice Book
Timeless Treasures

Name _____

▶ **Read the Vocabulary Words. Then use the Vocabulary Words to complete the webs.**

| navigation | mission | maneuver |
| high-tech | simulation | facilities |

1. _____

- steering
- flying
- charting a course

4. _____

- undertaking
- quest
- enterprise

2. _____

- launch pad
- training center
- communication building

5. _____

- pratice
- imitation
- model

3. _____

- sophisticated
- advanced
- lastest science

6. _____

- tactic
- operation
- exercise

 TRY THIS! Create a space log such as an astronaut might keep. Try to include Vocabulary Words in each entry.

Practice Book
Timeless Treasures

Name _____

► **Read the paragraph. Then circle the letter of the best answer to each question.**

Microbes, the tiny living things we often call germs, can live almost anywhere, even on the space station. Microbes get to outer space by hitchhiking on space-station materials and on astronauts. To eliminate microbes in the air, space-station air is kept very dry. The reason is that humid air promotes microbe growth.
To eliminate water-borne microbes, all water is heated and treated with iodine. These steps help to keep astronauts germ-free and in good health while they spend months in space.

1 How do microbes get on board the space station?

A The air is kept very dry.

B People call them germs.

C Iodine is added to water.

D They hitchhike on astronauts.

 Tip
Look for a sentence that contains the words *microbes* and *space station*.

2 What is the effect of heating water?

F Astronauts become ill.

G Water-borne microbes are eliminated.

H The water dries out.

J Microbe growth is promoted.

Tip
Heating water is the cause. To find the effect ask yourself, "What happens when the water is heated?"

3 What effect does treating the air and water lead to?

A spending months in space

B bringing microbes into the space station

C a germ-free environment for astronauts

D iodine in the air

Tip
Eliminate answers that cannot be found in the passage.

© Harcourt

SCHOOL-HOME CONNECTION Discuss with your child actions he or she can take to eliminate harmful microbes, or germs.

Practice Book
Timeless Treasures

Name _____

Skill Reminder • Use the **positive** form of an adverb when no comparison is being made. • Use the **comparative** form to compare one action with another action. • Use the **superlative** form to compare one action with two or more actions.

▶ **Underline the adverb in each sentence. Write whether it is *positive*, *comparative*, or *superlative*.**

1. Astronauts train more vigorously than most commercial pilots.

   _____

2. They may carefully examine substances for radioactivity. _____

3. Of all procedures, nose dives most accurately simulate the feeling of weightlessness.

   _____

4. Weightlessness causes astronauts to move more slowly around the space shuttle than

   they would in gravity. _____

5. Weightless objects float around less frequently when

   they are strapped down. _____

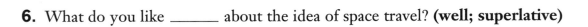

▶ **Rewrite each sentence, replacing the blank with the correct form of the adverb given in parentheses ( ).**

6. What do you like _____ about the idea of space travel? **(well; superlative)**

   _____

7. Do you move _____ on Earth, in space, or in water? **(slowly; superlative)**

   _____

8. You would probably sleep _____ in your bed than in space. **(soundly; comparative)**

   _____

TRY THIS! Imagine that you are an astronaut in space. Write a letter to a friend back home. Use one positive adverb, one comparative adverb, and one superlative adverb.

Name _____

Skill Reminder • Some words are often "clipped" to form a shorter word. • The shorter version, or clipped word, can be found at the beginning, middle, or end of the complete word.

▶ Fold the paper along the dotted line. As each spelling word is read aloud, write it in the blank. Then unfold your paper, and check your work. Practice spelling any words you missed.

1. _____
2. _____
3. _____
4. _____
5. _____
6. _____
7. _____
8. _____
9. _____
10. _____
11. _____
12. _____
13. _____
14. _____
15. _____
16. _____
17. _____
18. _____
19. _____
20. _____

SPELLING WORDS
1. luncheon
2. fanatic
3. advertisement
4. mathematics
5. caravan
6. bicycle
7. gasoline
8. hamburger
9. champion
10. gymnasium
11. Internet
12. microphone
13. influenza
14. embankment
15. dormitory
16. veterinarian
17. professional
18. automobile
19. laboratory
20. diskette

Practice Book
Timeless Treasures

© Harcourt

Name _____

▶ **Read the advertisement below, using context clues to determine the meanings of the boldfaced Vocabulary Words. Then write each Vocabulary Word next to its definition.**

TOO MUCH E-MAIL?   SILAS THE SORTER CAN HELP!

Are you being **bombarded** with tons of e-mail messages every day? Stop the cyber **barrage** with SILAS THE SORTER!

For only $25 per month, you can hire Silas to go to work for you every time you're **online.** Just hook him up to the **modem** that connects your computer to the Internet, and Silas will keep track of the **transmission** of e-mail messages to your address. He's fully **interactive,** so he'll ask you to tell him which messages to save and which to delete. All you do is click the mouse.

1. _____ the act of passing something along

2. _____ having two-way communication that involves a user's orders and responses

3. _____ an overwhelming attack of many things at once

4. _____ attacked repeatedly and rapidly

5. _____ connected to a computer network or the Internet

6. _____ an electronic device that allows computers to send messages over telephone lines or other lines

▶ **Write the Vocabulary Word that best completes each sentence.**

7. You might describe a huge amount of mail arriving at your home as a

_____.

8. If you are communicating with someone far away by computer, you must be

_____.

TRY THIS! Write a short message that includes an acronym, such as *modem.* Exchange messages with a partner.

© Harcourt

Practice Book
Timeless Treasures

▶ **Read the paragraph. Circle the letter of the best answer to each question.**

What does it mean to send e-mail in i-mode? Taryn has been reading about a new way to communicate that may make desktop computers obsolete. I-mode is already popular in Japan and probably will soon become popular everywhere. To use i-mode, you need a special wireless phone with a tiny screen. Although you can carry on conversations just as you would with any telephone, you can also send e-mail and surf the Web. It is even possible to download and play music. Taryn believes that i-mode may be the most exciting new technology ever.

1 Which of the following statements is a fact?

  A Desktop computers are out-of-date.

  B Telephone computers are exciting.

  C I-mode is a great way to send mail.

  D You can surf the Web in i-mode.

> 💡**Tip**
> Which statement is fact because it is based on observation or direct evidence?

2 Why is the last sentence in the paragraph an opinion?

  F It states Taryn's belief.

  G It is incorrect.

  H It is something Taryn can do.

  J It has to do with technology.

> 💡**Tip**
> In choosing your answer, think about what makes opinions different from facts.

3 Which fact does NOT support the opinion that i-mode will soon become popular everywhere?

  A Music can be downloaded and played in i-mode.

  B I-mode lets you talk on the telephone as well as surf the Web.

  C Taryn has been reading about i-mode communication.

  D I-mode lets you do many things on a tiny, portable screen.

> 💡**Tip**
> Choose the fact that does not give information about what might make i-mode popular.

SCHOOL-HOME CONNECTION With your child, discuss your opinions about computers. Then have your child write three sentences supporting his or her opinion with facts.

Skill Reminder	• **A preposition** shows the relationship

of a noun or a pronoun to another word in the sentence.

• **The noun or pronoun that follows a preposition is called the object of
the preposition.**

▶ **For each sentence, underline the complete prepositional phrase. Then write the
preposition and its object.**

1. Will you type an e-mail message for me?   _____

2. What is your address on the Internet?   _____

3. Have you ever sent a message to India?   _____

4. It is amazing that a message can be sent in seconds.   _____

5. An e-mail address does not have spaces between words. _____

▶ **Rewrite each sentence, replacing the blank with an appropriate preposition.**

6. How many hours a week do you spend _____ the Internet? _____

    _____

7. You can send a message _____ several people. _____

    _____

8. A bookmark is the address _____ a website. _____

    _____

9. If you click _____ the link, you will get to the site. _____

    _____

10. I surf the Net _____ the evening and _____ weekends. _____

    _____

**TRY
THIS!**   Scan the first five sentences of "CyberSurfer" for examples of prepositional
phrases. Write down any you find.

© Harcourt

Practice Book
Timeless Treasures

Skill Reminder Many English words have been borrowed from the French language.

▶ Fold the paper along the dotted line. As each spelling word is read aloud, write it in the blank. Then unfold your paper, and check your work. Practice spelling any words you missed.

1. _____
2. _____
3. _____
4. _____
5. _____
6. _____
7. _____
8. _____
9. _____
10. _____
11. _____
12. _____
13. _____
14. _____
15. _____
16. _____
17. _____
18. _____
19. _____
20. _____

SPELLING WORDS

1. envelope
2. croquet
3. beret
4. eclair
5. sacrifice
6. chalet
7. theater
8. parade
9. princess
10. bouquet
11. plateau
12. depot
13. etiquette
14. chauffeur
15. sergeant
16. ballet
17. cassette
18. campaign
19. cadet
20. camouflage

Practice Book
Timeless Treasures

Name _____

▶ **Use context clues to determine the meaning of the boldfaced Vocabulary Word in each sentence. Then write the Vocabulary Word that completes each analogy.**

The scientist made a **breakthrough** that led to advances in space travel.
The **satellite** orbited Earth twice each day.
The **cosmonaut** set a record for the most time spent at a space station.
Shawn **disregarded** his fear of heights and went ahead with flight training.
Sara **enrolls** in space camp this spring so she can attend this summer.
Rocket fuel is made from special **formulas** designed to provide a lot of power.
The **altimeter** showed that the spacecraft was 100 miles up in space.
When the launch was canceled, the crew left the spacecraft **dejectedly.**

1. *Happy* is to *cheerfully* as *sad* is to _____.

2. *Racetrack* is to *race car* as *orbit* is to _____.

3. *American* is to *astronaut* as *Russian* is to _____.

4. *Temperature* is to *thermometer* as *height* is to _____.

5. *Ingredients* are to *recipes* as *elements* are to _____.

6. *Listened* is to *heard* as *ignored* is to _____.

7. *Fails* is to *passes* as *drops* is to _____.

8. *Important* is to *significant* as *discovery* is to _____.

▶ **Answer each question, and give a reason for your answer. Use a Vocabulary Word in your answer.**

9. What scientific **breakthrough** would you most like to be made next?

_____

_____

10. Is the expense of sending a **satellite** into space worthwhile?

_____

_____

Name _____

▶ **Read the paragraph. Then circle the letter of the best answer to each question.**

The *Sputniks* were a series of satellites launched by the former Soviet Union. *Sputnik 1* was launched on October 4, 1957. This lightweight satellite lasted only until early 1958, when it fell back to Earth and burned. Yet it would be hard to exaggerate its importance. *Sputnik 1* began the Space Age and the massive efforts of the United States to catch up to its rival. Many *Sputniks* were to follow in the next few years. *Sputnik 2* carried the dog Laika, the first creature in space. Eight other *Sputniks* gathered volumes of information on space.

1 What conclusion can you draw about why *Sputnik 1* was so important?

A It found out lots of information about space.

B It was launched by the former Soviet Union.

C *Sputnik 1* was the first satellite to orbit Earth.

D It carried a dog into space.

> **💡 Tip**
> Make sure to draw your conclusion based on information on *Sputnik 1*, not other *Sputniks* in the program.

2 What evidence supports the conclusion that the *Sputnik* program was successful?

F *Sputnik 2* carried a dog into space.

G Many *Sputniks* orbited Earth and gathered data.

H Eight *Sputniks* are orbiting Earth and collecting data.

J More *Sputniks* will soon be launched.

> **💡 Tip**
> Remember to base your answer on information in the text as well as what you may already know about the topic.

3 Which conclusion can you draw about the effect of *Sputnik 1* on the United States?

A *Sputnik 1* didn't have much of an effect on the United States.

B *Sputnik 1* caused the United States to begin a huge space program.

C *Sputnik 1* interested many students in the United States.

D *Sputnik 1* caused the United States to begin exploring the oceans.

> **💡 Tip**
> The former Soviet Union and the U.S. were bitter rivals when the *Sputnik* program began. This knowledge should help you answer the question.

© Harcourt

SCHOOL-HOME CONNECTION Discuss space exploration with your child. Share any memories you have of important events in space.

131

Practice Book
Timeless Treasures

Name _____

The Case of the
Shining Blue
Planet

Grammar:
Adjective and
Adverb Phrases

Skill Reminder • An **adjective phrase** is a prepositional phrase that modifies a noun or a pronoun. An adjective phrase tells *what kind, how many,* or *which one.* • An **adverb phrase** is a prepositional phrase that modifies a verb, an adjective, or another adverb. An adverb phrase tells *how, when, where, to what extent,* or *how often.*

▶ **Underline each adjective phrase. Circle each adverb phrase.**

1. Many of the cosmonauts were Russian.

2. They trained with great diligence.

3. The cosmonauts practiced routine maneuvers

   before the launch.

4. They became experts in weightless environments.

▶ **Write the phrase in each sentence. Label the adjective phrases *adj* and the adverb phrases *adv.* Tell which word the phrase modifies.**

5. The cosmonauts gathered on the launch pad.

   _____

6. They waved to the nervous spectators.

   _____

7. Many of the spectators held their breath.

   _____

8. Then everyone in the observation area cheered.

   _____

 TRY THIS! Continue the account of the launch. Use at least one adjective phrase and one adverb phrase in your account.

Practice Book
Timeless Treasures

© Harcourt

Name _____

Skill Reminder • The spelling and pronunciation of a base
word often changes when a related word is formed. • To spell a
related word, divide it into syllables and look for familiar spelling patterns.

▶ Fold the paper along the dotted line. As each spelling word is read aloud, write it
in the blank. Then unfold your paper, and check your work. Practice spelling any
words you missed.

1. _____

2. _____

3. _____

4. _____

5. _____

6. _____

7. _____

8. _____

9. _____

10. _____

11. _____

12. _____

13. _____

14. _____

15. _____

16. _____

17. _____

18. _____

19. _____

20. _____

SPELLING WORDS

1. real
2. reality
3. precise
4. precision
5. similar
6. similarity
7. conserve
8. conservation
9. sign
10. signature
11. family
12. familiar
13. satisfy
14. satisfactory
15. commerce
16. commercial
17. define
18. definition
19. reduce
20. reduction

Practice Book
Timeless Treasures

Skills and Strategies Index

Skills and Strategies Index

LITERARY RESPONSE AND ANALYSIS

SPELLING

RESEARCH AND INFORMATION SKILLS

VOCABULARY

Practice Book
Timeless Treasures

• T R O P H I E S •

End-of-Selection Tests

Grade 6

The Best School Year Ever

Directions: For items 1–18, fill in the circle in front of the correct answer. For items 19–20, write the answer.

Vocabulary

1. It's always nice to receive a _____ for work well done.
   - Ⓐ mishap
   - Ⓑ compliment
   - Ⓒ terminal
   - Ⓓ criticism

2. Students can sometimes be _____ in thinking of reasons why their homework isn't done.
   - Ⓐ inventive
   - Ⓑ inviting
   - Ⓒ visible
   - Ⓓ detective

3. Brad has a _____ that I admire, and that is honesty.
   - Ⓐ conversation
   - Ⓑ community
   - Ⓒ quality
   - Ⓓ compliant

4. I almost collapsed with _____ when I accidentally tripped and fell down in front of the whole class.
   - Ⓐ embarrassment
   - Ⓑ penalty
   - Ⓒ revival
   - Ⓓ patience

5. Karen has shown that she is _____ in an emergency, often coming up with clever ideas to save the day.
   - Ⓐ distorted
   - Ⓑ resourceful
   - Ⓒ addresses
   - Ⓓ ignited

6. Selling sandwiches at lunch proved to be an _____ project for our class.
   - Ⓐ enterprising
   - Ⓑ admired
   - Ⓒ assignment
   - Ⓓ understand

7. The owner of the big market is known for making _____ deals.
   - Ⓐ amount
   - Ⓑ generations
   - Ⓒ shrewd
   - Ⓓ launching

Comprehension

8. Why does Miss Kemp say that the last day of school is important for the students this year?

(A) They will find out who has the most compliments.

(B) They will learn things about themselves and about each other.

(C) They will see who has drawn each other's name.

(D) They are trying to be nice to each other.

9. Why has it been hard to find compliments for Imogene?

(A) She is very quiet.

(B) There aren't any words to describe her actions.

(C) It is difficult to know when she does something good.

(D) She is not good at sports.

10. According to the narrator, what is one good thing that Imogene had done?

(A) She had told Boyd that they would save a little of his ears.

(B) She had gotten Boyd's head out of the bike rack.

(C) She had taped Boyd's ears out of the way.

(D) She had walked Boyd home.

11. Who had scared Boyd the most?

(A) Mr. Crabtree

(B) Gladys Herdman

(C) Imogene Herdman

(D) Jolene Liggett

12. Why had Boyd believed that someone might cut off his ears?

(A) He thinks like a first grader.

(B) His ears are big.

(C) The firemen had told him so.

(D) His mother had told him so.

© Harcourt

Practice Book
Timeless Treasures

13. Who is the narrator?
   (A) Ollie
   (B) Gladys
   (C) Beth
   (D) Louella

14. How does Imogene react when it's time to hear what the narrator wrote about her?
   (A) Imogene is eager to hear the compliments.
   (B) Imogene is confident that the narrator will say good things.
   (C) Imogene is unconcerned about it.
   (D) Imogene doesn't want to hear what the narrator wrote.

15. Alice claims Beth's compliments about Imogene are _____ .
   (A) not nice
   (B) copied from the dictionary
   (C) creative
   (D) very fitting

16. Why does Alice say that Beth makes Imogene sound like a wonderful person?
   (A) Alice thinks that Beth's compliments about Imogene are not true.
   (B) Alice and Imogene are worst enemies.
   (C) Beth uses humorous words to describe Imogene.
   (D) Beth uses many words that mean "resourceful."

17. What does Imogene do after she hears the words Beth uses?
   (A) She writes them in a notebook.
   (B) She just forgets about them.
   (C) She shoves a Magic Marker at Beth.
   (D) She brags to everyone that she is resourceful.

Practice Book
Timeless Treasures

18. Why does Imogene shove a Magic Marker at Beth?

Ⓐ Imogene keeps notes to herself on her arm.

Ⓑ She likes having writing on her arm.

Ⓒ She wants Beth to write "resourceful" on her arm.

Ⓓ Imogene wants to get Gladys.

19. How does Beth feel about Imogene at the beginning of the story? at the end?

_____

_____

_____

_____

_____

_____

_____

20. Miss Kemp asks the students, "Which was harder—to give compliments or to receive them?" What did the class say? Do you agree with the class? Why or why not?

_____

_____

_____

_____

_____

_____

_____

Yang the Eldest and His Odd Jobs

Directions: For items 1–18, fill in the circle in front of the correct answer. For items 19–20, write the answer.

Vocabulary

1. The farmers sell flowers in the covered _____ of the outdoor market.
   - Ⓐ affordable
   - Ⓑ arcade
   - Ⓒ collection
   - Ⓓ crusty

2. Every Saturday the _____ display their goods at the open air market.
   - Ⓐ profits
   - Ⓑ quality
   - Ⓒ vendors
   - Ⓓ purchasers

3. The audience laughed and laughed at the _____ jokes the comedian told.
   - Ⓐ inventive
   - Ⓑ urgent
   - Ⓒ strange
   - Ⓓ hilarious

4. After my brother joined his good friends at the game, his _____ disappeared.
   - Ⓐ sulkiness
   - Ⓑ carelessness
   - Ⓒ strangeness
   - Ⓓ disposition

5. The band director ended the Sousa march with a _____ of his baton in the air.
   - Ⓐ flourish
   - Ⓑ vision
   - Ⓒ vanish
   - Ⓓ frequency

Practice Book
Timeless Treasures

6. Attending a concert in the afternoon is a _____ because most concerts are in the evening.

(A) royalty

(B) novelty

(C) distance

(D) fountain

7. My brother feels grown-up because this is the first roller coaster ride he has gone on _____ by an adult.

(A) uncooperative

(B) collected

(C) unaccompanied

(D) accustomed

Comprehension

8. The narrator of the selection admires his eldest brother because _____ .

(A) he can do nothing well

(B) babysitting is difficult for him

(C) he can do almost anything well

(D) he wanted to earn extra money

9. When the brothers attend Pike Place Market, they _____ .

(A) purchase flowers for their mother

(B) see an organ grinder with a monkey

(C) remember the open air markets in China

(D) see people throw flowers into the instrument cases

10. At first, how does Eldest Brother feel about playing music at Pike Place Market?

(A) It would be entertaining.

(B) It's like playing at a concert and getting paid.

(C) It's like begging.

(D) He needs a dog to stand by him and bark.

© Harcourt

Practice Book
Timeless Treasures

11. "Stars and Stripes Forever" is usually played by marching bands because it is a lively _____ .

Ⓐ sonata

Ⓑ march

Ⓒ waltz

Ⓓ symphony

12. Eldest Brother doesn't hang around with people his own age because he _____ .

Ⓐ is lonely

Ⓑ is concentrating on his music

Ⓒ works many jobs

Ⓓ doesn't like people his own age

13. Playing at Pike Place Market is not successful because _____ .

Ⓐ there is too much competition there

Ⓑ people do not like Elder Brother's music

Ⓒ everyone is attending the Fremont street fair

Ⓓ there aren't enough people there

14. Summers in Seattle are usually dry, but they are _____ .

Ⓐ always hot and sunny

Ⓑ always cloudless and windy

Ⓒ often cloudy

Ⓓ often hot and humid

15. How does Fourth Brother keep Eldest Brother's sheet music from blowing away?

Ⓐ Fourth Brother holds the music.

Ⓑ Eldest Brother plays pieces he doesn't need music for.

Ⓒ Fourth Brother nails the music to the music stand.

Ⓓ Fourth Brother clips the music to the stand with clothespins.

Practice Book
Timeless Treasures

16. How does the narrator react to the juggler?

   Ⓐ He thinks his act is really terrific.

   Ⓑ He finds the juggler's white face scary.

   Ⓒ He is afraid the juggler will start a fire with the lighted torches.

   Ⓓ He wants Eldest Brother to juggle, too.

17. When Eldest Brother plays "The Flower Drum Song," the narrator _____ .

   Ⓐ sings the words

   Ⓑ whistles the tune

   Ⓒ drums along on an ice cream bucket

   Ⓓ counts all the money

18. How does Eldest Brother feel about Lisa's musical ability?

   Ⓐ jealous

   Ⓑ that she's talented for her age

   Ⓒ that she's no competition for him

   Ⓓ that she's superior to him

19. Why does Eldest Brother play an Irish jig?

_____

_____

_____

_____

_____

20. How does Eldest Brother eventually make money?

_____

_____

_____

_____

_____

Knots in My Yo-yo String

Directions: For items 1–18, fill in the circle in front of the correct answer. For items 19–20, write the answer.

Vocabulary

1. I don't like having you _____ at me with such an evil look in your eyes.
- Ⓐ infect
- Ⓑ pretend
- Ⓒ glare
- Ⓓ improve

2. That politician is _____ to win the election.
- Ⓐ favored
- Ⓑ convicted
- Ⓒ organize
- Ⓓ restricted

3. As a _____ of their trip, the tour guide gave the people on the tour a small souvenir.
- Ⓐ vaccine
- Ⓑ memento
- Ⓒ career
- Ⓓ concern

4. The coach shook the hands of the players to _____ them over the loss of the game.
- Ⓐ persist
- Ⓑ satisfy
- Ⓒ define
- Ⓓ console

5. Many athletes reach their _____ performances in their thirties.
- Ⓐ aware
- Ⓑ peak
- Ⓒ tear
- Ⓓ croak

6. The riders _____ on their horses off into the woods.

   Ⓐ trotted   Ⓑ checked

   Ⓒ rippled   Ⓓ wrecked

7. Most people are _____ to polio because they received the vaccine.

   Ⓐ immerged   Ⓑ immune

   Ⓒ warned   Ⓓ exposed

Comprehension

8. What is the narrator's most prized memento from grade-school days?

   Ⓐ a trophy for playing shortstop

   Ⓑ a medal for the 50-yard dash

   Ⓒ his father's stopwatch

   Ⓓ the sneakers he wore in a real race

9. When the narrator was in his teens, what did he want to be when he grew up?

   Ⓐ a first baseman

   Ⓑ a long distance runner

   Ⓒ a shortstop

   Ⓓ an umpire

10. How does this selection say the Little League gives more kids a chance to participate?

   Ⓐ Kids share uniforms.

   Ⓑ Volunteers drive kids to the games.

   Ⓒ The league organizes more teams.

   Ⓓ Kids take turns playing on different teams.

11. How does the narrator feel when he makes his first error during a game?

   Ⓐ He doesn't care because it is his first error.

   Ⓑ He is disappointed and angry with himself.

   Ⓒ He is disgusted and angry with the batter.

   Ⓓ He can't believe he caught it.

12. What lesson does the narrator learn from his first error?

Ⓐ Always try for a home run.

Ⓑ Be proud about good fielding.

Ⓒ Practice more and pay attention.

Ⓓ Take action instead of feeling sorry for yourself.

13. According to the narrator, his first history book was _____ .

Ⓐ *The Philadelphia Inquirer*

Ⓑ the baseball encyclopedia

Ⓒ the baseball almanac

Ⓓ *American History Before 1960*

14. According to the narrator, why is a trophy a better reward than a jacket?

Ⓐ It says State Champions on the back of the jacket.

Ⓑ A trophy doesn't wear out.

Ⓒ He can take a trophy home.

Ⓓ He doesn't think a jacket is anything special to show for a triumph.

15. Besides playing baseball, what does the narrator do as part of his love for the game?

Ⓐ study batting averages

Ⓑ buy a new glove

Ⓒ mow the grass on the diamond

Ⓓ repeat the Sportsmanship Pledge at every game

16. According to the selection, why are taped baseballs used in most sandlot games?

Ⓐ Taped balls fly farther when hit.

Ⓑ Taped balls are easier to see.

Ⓒ The horsehide cover protects a baseball only in shipping.

Ⓓ Baseballs are used so much that the original covers come off.

17. According to the narrator, one way to practice being a shortstop is
to _____ .
(A) practice batting and catching with his dad
(B) play at Connie Mack Stadium
(C) bounce tennis balls off brick walls and then catch them
(D) study the batting averages of major league players

18. Why is this selection considered nonfiction?
(A) The selection is written using the word *I*.
(B) No one can make up facts like the ones in this selection.
(C) Norristown, Pennsylvania, is a real place.
(D) The narrator is recalling events that really happened.

19. Write the steps, in the correct order, that the narrator follows at the end of
the baseball season.

_____

_____

_____

_____

_____

_____

20. How does the narrator spend the six months between baseball seasons?

_____

_____

_____

_____

_____

_____

Directions: For items 1–18, fill in the circle in front of the correct answer. For items 19–20, write the answer.

Vocabulary

1. Lucy _____ through the piles of books in hopes of finding one she hadn't read.
Ⓐ resisted
Ⓑ suspected
Ⓒ pleaded
Ⓓ rummaged

2. I admitted our error _____, only after I realized I had no other choice.
Ⓐ expertly
Ⓑ intensively
Ⓒ reluctantly
Ⓓ sternly

3. The golfer _____ her arms before she teed off.
Ⓐ flexed
Ⓒ flourished
Ⓑ invented
Ⓓ trotted

4. Maria _____ when she had to do her assignment again because she lost her homework.
Ⓐ favored
Ⓒ fumed
Ⓑ agreed
Ⓓ pretended

5. After the puppy had chased the ball, it collapsed on the floor from _____ .
Ⓐ question
Ⓒ exhaustion
Ⓑ embarrassment
Ⓓ celebration

6. Animals have a natural _____ that warns them when danger is near.
Ⓐ immunity
Ⓒ compliment
Ⓑ silkiness
Ⓓ instinct

Comprehension

7. This selection can be described as a short story because of all the following reasons **except** that the story _____ .

   Ⓐ has a problem and solves it

   Ⓑ has a theme and creates a mood

   Ⓒ does not depend on illustrations

   Ⓓ contains images and is like a poem

8. Why isn't Lupe Medrano good at sports?

   Ⓐ People can't be smart and good in sports.

   Ⓑ She doesn't have good coordination.

   Ⓒ She is a shy person.

   Ⓓ She has a razor-sharp mind.

9. Why does Lupe want to be good at a sport?

   Ⓐ She likes to win awards but has no sports awards.

   Ⓑ She doesn't like being smart.

   Ⓒ She wants more trophies than anyone else.

   Ⓓ She doesn't like playing sports.

10. Why does Lupe pick marbles for her sport?

   Ⓐ She can play with her brother's marbles.

   Ⓑ No one else plays marbles.

   Ⓒ She learns to aim a marble accurately.

   Ⓓ It is the easiest sport.

11. How does Lupe's brother show that he is a good sport?

   Ⓐ by letting her beat him

   Ⓑ by giving her tips on how to shoot

   Ⓒ by showing her how to beat Alfonso

   Ⓓ by letting her have his marbles

12. Alfonso says, "Man, she's bad! She can beat the other girls. . . ." He means that Lupe is _____ .

Ⓐ not a nice person

Ⓑ a very good marble player

Ⓒ not as good as her brother

Ⓓ not doing well in school

13. What does Mr. Medrano do to encourage his daughter's interest in sports?

Ⓐ makes jokes about her big thumb

Ⓑ tells Lupe that she is good at sports

Ⓒ helps Lupe beat her brother at marbles

Ⓓ goes to watch her play marbles

14. Mr. Medrano tells Lupe, "Just think of the marbles, not the girl, and let your thumb do the work." What does he mean?

Ⓐ Your opponent will not win, so pay no attention to her.

Ⓑ Don't talk to the girl about the game.

Ⓒ Don't worry about your opponent. Just concentrate on your game.

Ⓓ Your opponent doesn't have your thumb.

15. How does Lupe react after she beats the girl in the baseball cap?

Ⓐ Lupe shakes hands with her.

Ⓑ Lupe brags to everyone.

Ⓒ Lupe asks a photographer to take pictures of the two of them.

Ⓓ Lupe walks away quietly.

16. Why is the girl in the baseball cap Lupe's toughest opponent?

Ⓐ She looks very serious.

Ⓑ She is a very good player.

Ⓒ She is a poor loser.

Ⓓ She wins the first marble.

Practice Book
Timeless Treasures

17. Which word best describes Lupe?

Ⓐ determined

Ⓑ show-off

Ⓒ kind

Ⓓ easily upset

18. Which word best describes how Lupe feels back home after winning the marble championship?

Ⓐ tired

Ⓑ proud

Ⓒ embarrassed

Ⓓ persistent

19. How does Lupe's family celebrate her victory?

_____

_____

_____

_____

_____

20. How are Jerry's athletic goals in "Knots in my Yo-yo String" and Lupe's goals different?

_____

_____

_____

_____

_____

_____

_____

Practice Book
Timeless Treasures

Directions: For items 1–18, fill in the circle in front of the correct answer. For items 19–20, write the answer.

Vocabulary

1. We all want to erect the statue, but _____ such a project will be costly.
   - Ⓐ colliding
   - Ⓑ irritating
   - Ⓒ funding
   - Ⓓ curing

2. Any _____ of the city building codes will result in steep fines.
   - Ⓐ violations
   - Ⓑ measure
   - Ⓒ legends
   - Ⓓ trends

3. Lowering ticket prices proved to be an _____ way to get more people to attend our shows.
   - Ⓐ irrigated
   - Ⓑ effective
   - Ⓒ extinct
   - Ⓓ insisted

4. Because it is still raining, we will have to _____ our baseball game.
   - Ⓐ dilute
   - Ⓑ pollute
   - Ⓒ postpone
   - Ⓓ reside

5. The topic of additional playground equipment is the first item on the _____ for the town meeting.
   - Ⓐ summons
   - Ⓑ agenda
   - Ⓒ permission
   - Ⓓ attention

6. Our town has an _____ that no dogs are allowed on the beach during the day.
   - Ⓐ compliment
   - Ⓑ flourish
   - Ⓒ profession
   - Ⓓ ordinance

7. The board members will listen to arguments from both sides on the important _____ .
   - Ⓐ issue
   - Ⓑ include
   - Ⓒ education
   - Ⓓ particle

Comprehension

8. Linda Gold feels teaching is a difficult profession. All the following statements support her feeling about teaching **except** _____ .
   - (A) teachers need all the support they can get
   - (B) education is the key to a good and secure future
   - (C) homeless people don't know how to farm
   - (D) teachers help students get an education

9. Sweeby Jones says that there is something wrong with people if they _____ .
   - (A) are homeless
   - (B) are hungry and can't feed themselves
   - (C) want a basketball court instead of a garden
   - (D) don't mind other people being hungry

10. In his newspaper article, what does Darnell Rock say is the value of a garden for the homeless?
   - (A) It is a chance for people to help themselves.
   - (B) It is a place where homeless people can live and feed themselves.
   - (C) It is better than a basketball court.
   - (D) It is a way for the city to help kids.

11. What does Darnell Rock believe about a person's life?
   - (A) Anyone can plan completely how his or her life will work out.
   - (B) What you do with your life is what is most important.
   - (C) If you are born poor, then you will be poor for the rest of your life.
   - (D) Sometimes a person deserves to be homeless.

12. What is the main reason that Linda Gold wrote an article in support of a parking lot for teachers?
   - (A) Homeless people don't have experience farming.
   - (B) Homeless people aren't good examples of how to live, but teachers are.
   - (C) Teachers need all the support they can get.
   - (D) Having a garden on the old basketball court is a bad idea that helps nobody.

13. According to Darnell, how can a garden for the homeless help kids?

Ⓐ It may help kids think about what they're doing or not doing with their lives.

Ⓑ A garden for the homeless will help kids stay out of trouble.

Ⓒ The kids can help the homeless learn how to grow their own food.

Ⓓ The kids can learn how to tend a garden.

14. How does the councilman seem to feel when Mr. Sweeby speaks in the meeting?

Ⓐ bored

Ⓑ angry

Ⓒ confused

Ⓓ disgusted

15. Mr. Sweeby says that he wishes that Darnell had been his friend when he was Darnell's age. What does Mr. Sweeby mean?

Ⓐ Sweeby likes Darnell.

Ⓑ Sweeby would be smart and successful.

Ⓒ If Darnell had been his friend, Sweeby would be a councilman.

Ⓓ Having Darnell as a friend might have changed his life.

16. How does Darnell feel when the council votes against the garden?

Ⓐ He wishes he had not made a speech.

Ⓑ He thinks that he has let Sweeby down.

Ⓒ He doesn't understand why he lost.

Ⓓ He is angry at Linda Gold.

17. The photographers want Darnell to be part of the ground breaking. In this selection, *ground breaking* means _____ .

Ⓐ digging the first shovel of earth at a ceremony

Ⓑ being seen with the mayor at a ceremony

Ⓒ digging the garden before the mayor speaks

Ⓓ clearing space for the garden

18. What is Sweeby's good news?

 Ⓐ He is going to talk to the City Council.

 Ⓑ A garden is planned for Jackson Avenue.

 Ⓒ He and some friends are renting an apartment together.

 Ⓓ He has a job at a hospital and a place to live.

19. What does Sweeby mean when he says that the garden is going to make a big difference?

_____

_____

_____

_____

_____

_____

_____

_____

20. Sweeby says that his new job is a small start. What does he mean?

_____

_____

_____

_____

_____

_____

_____

_____

Number the Stars

Directions: For items 1–18, fill in the circle in front of the correct answer. For items 19–20, write the answer.

Vocabulary

1. Jeff tried to calm the frightened horse by talking _____ to it.
   - Ⓐ mistakenly
   - Ⓑ soothingly
   - Ⓒ confusingly
   - Ⓓ doubtingly

2. Alicia stood her ground and spoke in a strong and _____ voice.
   - Ⓐ unwavering
   - Ⓑ unclaimed
   - Ⓒ unsightly
   - Ⓓ uncapped

3. During World War II, Denmark was under German _____ .
   - Ⓐ profession
   - Ⓑ violation
   - Ⓒ exhaustion
   - Ⓓ occupation

4. I was so _____ with my dog after he chewed on my new sneakers that I didn't play with him all day.
   - Ⓐ enthroned
   - Ⓑ exasperated
   - Ⓒ enchanted
   - Ⓓ extracted

5. The soldiers spoke to the captives _____ when they did not march fast enough.
   - Ⓐ disdainfully
   - Ⓑ dramatically
   - Ⓒ obediently
   - Ⓓ scornful

6. The teenagers argued _____ with the teacher when they learned that they could not go on the class trip without a permission slip.
   - Ⓐ cheerfully
   - Ⓑ currently
   - Ⓒ belligerently
   - Ⓓ briskly

Comprehension

7. Where does this selection take place?
   - (A) in Germany
   - (B) in America
   - (C) in Denmark
   - (D) in Tivoli Gardens

8. Why does Mrs. Johansen buy fish skin shoes?
   - (A) Kirsti likes new things.
   - (B) They are the only shoes available because of the war.
   - (C) She likes the color of the shoes.
   - (D) She doesn't think Kirsti will mind green shoes.

9. Ellen solves Kirsti's shoe problem by _____ .
   - (A) promising to help Kirsti get a different pair of shoes
   - (B) suggesting that Kirsti give the shoes away
   - (C) offering to have her father blacken them
   - (D) offering to trade her shoes with Kirsti

10. What event happened on Kirsti's birthday?
    - (A) Kirsti saw fireworks for the first time.
    - (B) Tivoli Gardens burned.
    - (C) The Johansens celebrated at Tivoli Gardens.
    - (D) The Danes destroyed their naval fleet.

11. Why did the Danes blow up their naval fleet?
    - (A) The war was over and they didn't need the ships.
    - (B) It was the night before the beginning of the Jewish New Year.
    - (C) The Danes didn't want the Germans to be able to use their ships.
    - (D) They wanted to have a large fireworks display.

12. What news does Mr. Johansen explain to Annemarie?

   (A) that the Nazis plan to arrest all Danish Jews

   (B) that Ellen is going to live with the Johansens

   (C) that Mr. and Mrs. Rosen are at Ellen's grandmother's house

   (D) that the Johansens and the Rosens are leaving Copenhagen

13. Why can't the Rosens celebrate the Jewish New Year?

   (A) They do not have food or candles.

   (B) No one can come to their house.

   (C) They have to visit some relatives.

   (D) They have to hide from the Nazis.

14. What does Mr. Johansen promise Ellen?

   (A) that the rabbi is taking care of her parents

   (B) that she will be happy living with Annemarie

   (C) that her parents are safe and that she will see them again

   (D) that no one knows where her parents are hiding

15. Who is Ellen pretending to be when the soldiers come?

   (A) Annemarie

   (B) Annemarie's dead sister

   (C) Annemarie's younger sister

   (D) a friend of the Johansens

16. When the Nazis are at the Johansens' home, how does the family feel?

   (A) tense and fearful

   (B) curious and interested

   (C) angry and frustrated

   (D) tired and annoyed

17. This selection is mainly about _____ .

   (A) a Danish family hiding a Jewish girl from German soldiers

   (B) two sisters who are pretending to be friends

   (C) Mr. Johansen hiding the Rosens from the German soldiers

   (D) the Rosens moving away from the Johansens

18. In what section of the library would you most likely find this book?

   Ⓐ fiction

   Ⓑ drama

   Ⓒ mysteries

   Ⓓ nonfiction

19. Why is the Star of David necklace so important?

_____

_____

_____

_____

_____

_____

_____

_____

20. What does Mr. Johansen do to save Ellen from the soldiers? Why does this act save her?

_____

_____

_____

_____

_____

_____

_____

_____

_____

The Summer of the Swans

Directions: For items 1–18, fill in the circle in front of the correct answer. For items 19–20, write the answer.

Vocabulary

1. Shocked that she had won the award, Keisha stared at the judges with _____ .
   - (A) discord
   - (B) disbelief
   - (C) disaster
   - (D) discipline

2. Roy looked out at the vast _____ of land and wondered how he would ever get it plowed and planted.
   - (A) crevice
   - (B) penalty
   - (C) expanse
   - (D) details

3. I was suddenly overcome by a _____ to do something silly.
   - (A) compulsion
   - (B) connection
   - (C) compression
   - (D) complexion

4. The _____ of being lost in the woods was the worst experience of the little boy's whole life.
   - (A) famine
   - (B) novelty
   - (C) inventiveness
   - (D) anguish

Name _____ **Date** _____

5. Lost in the storm and missing its mother, the calf _____ loudly.
- Ⓐ relaxed
- Ⓑ wailed
- Ⓒ admitted
- Ⓓ waved

6. The girl's voice began to _____ before she broke into tears.
- Ⓐ decline
- Ⓑ season
- Ⓒ enlist
- Ⓓ waver

7. The crashing waves threaten to _____ the tiny island.
- Ⓐ engulf
- Ⓑ entertain
- Ⓒ enjoy
- Ⓓ enlist

Comprehension

8. Why does Charlie feel hopeless?
- Ⓐ He misses his sister.
- Ⓑ He is afraid of the chipmunk.
- Ⓒ He is lost.
- Ⓓ He has lost his watch stem.

9. When does Charlie cry and scream?
- Ⓐ when he sees some shadows
- Ⓑ after he cannot find the chipmunk's hole
- Ⓒ when he hears strange noises
- Ⓓ before he gets dirt under his fingernails from digging in the earth

10. Sara and Joe hope that they can see Charlie from the _____ .
- Ⓐ top of the hill
- Ⓑ lake
- Ⓒ cow pasture
- Ⓓ school parking lot

11. What does Sara think that Charlie likes to do?
- (A) play actor and actress
- (B) watch the afternoon movie
- (C) look at Aunt Willie's jewel box
- (D) pretend he is in game shows

12. Why doesn't Sara cry while she is calling for Charlie?
- (A) She won't hear Charlie if she is crying.
- (B) She can't bear the thought of never seeing him again.
- (C) She thinks crying is a waste of time.
- (D) She has used up all her tears on things that aren't important.

13. What happens often to Charlie?
- (A) He cannot remember events.
- (B) He can't find his slippers.
- (C) He gets lost in Aunt Willie's house.
- (D) He falls asleep in the forest.

14. Charlie feels safest when _____ .
- (A) there is a big surprise waiting for him
- (B) he follows his usual way of doing things
- (C) Aunt Willie puts him to bed
- (D) he is by himself

15. When does Charlie begin to shout excitedly?
- (A) after he hears someone calling his name
- (B) when he sees a bird sitting on a branch
- (C) after his body starts aching
- (D) just before thinking about Aunt Willie's cigar box

16. What is the first thing that Charlie does when he sees Sara?
- (A) asks to go home
- (B) has Sara wind his watch
- (C) looks at her in disbelief and joy
- (D) closes his eyes and clutches her shirt

17. Why is Charlie's watch so important to him?

Ⓐ He is just learning to tell time.

Ⓑ He likes to watch the second hand go around and around.

Ⓒ He wants to know if he's missed his favorite television program.

Ⓓ It is a familiar part of his daily routine.

18. What experience has Sara had that helps her to understand Charlie's feelings when he is lost?

Ⓐ She was lost at school and became frightened.

Ⓑ She had fallen into the same ravine where Charlie was.

Ⓒ She had a high fever with the measles and could not find her way back to bed.

Ⓓ She was hit in the face with a baseball and became disoriented.

19. List two reasons why Sara gives Charlie his slipper.

_____

_____

_____

_____

_____

20. Charlie asks Sara to wind his watch. What doesn't he understand about the watch?

_____

_____

_____

_____

_____

_____

_____

Old Yeller

Directions: For items 1–18, fill in the circle in front of the correct answer. For items 19–20, write the answer.

Vocabulary

1. The playful kitten _____ on the ball of string and began to unravel it.
   - (A) planned
   - (B) disgraced
   - (C) declined
   - (D) pounced

2. I have heard some strange _____ in my day, but your story is the least believable of all.
   - (A) yeast
   - (B) yarns
   - (C) wrinkles
   - (D) miniatures

3. The angry bull was _____ toward the bull rider, intent on running him down.
   - (A) adorning
   - (B) concerning
   - (C) charging
   - (D) docking

4. The horse was _____ forward with such force that it almost threw its rider.
   - (A) lunging
   - (B) lilting
   - (C) acting
   - (D) funding

5. Everyone was _____ when it seemd like the rain would not stop.
   - (A) screwdriver
   - (B) peak
   - (C) waver
   - (D) frantic

6. The baby cubs were _____ and playing in the lake until the mother bear saw a snake.
   - (A) enterprising
   - (B) captured
   - (C) romping
   - (D) drown

Practice Book
Timeless Treasures

Comprehension

7. Why is Arliss always getting into trouble?
   - Ⓐ He tries to catch any creature that he sees.
   - Ⓑ He never listens to his mother.
   - Ⓒ He is always telling imaginary stories about what happened.
   - Ⓓ He goes wherever Old Yeller goes.

8. Why does Arliss believe that he can catch any animal around his home?
   - Ⓐ Old Yeller is smart and loves Arliss.
   - Ⓑ Arliss is very smart and a good hunter.
   - Ⓒ Arliss always gets any animal he goes after.
   - Ⓓ Old Yeller catches animals, and Arliss pretends he has caught them.

9. The narrator says that Arliss "told the biggest windy I ever heard." In this selection, a *windy* is _____ .
   - Ⓐ a big gale
   - Ⓑ a very exaggerated story
   - Ⓒ a tale told by a little boy
   - Ⓓ the ability to hold your breath for a long time

10. Arliss has caught all the animals listed below **except** _____ .
    - Ⓐ snakes
    - Ⓑ mountain lions
    - Ⓒ rabbits
    - Ⓓ tree lizards

11. What happens to Arliss when he catches a blue catfish?
    - Ⓐ The fish gets away.
    - Ⓑ Arliss falls into Birdsong Creek.
    - Ⓒ The fish fins him.
    - Ⓓ Arliss turns the fish loose.

12. Where does this selection take place?

Ⓐ in Texas

Ⓑ in Mexico

Ⓒ in Minnesota

Ⓓ in Arizona

13. How are Travis and Arliss alike?

Ⓐ They are good hunters.

Ⓑ They are always getting into trouble.

Ⓒ Both children have told whoppers.

Ⓓ Both have a stubborn streak.

14. What is Arliss constantly doing?

Ⓐ swimming

Ⓑ climbing

Ⓒ screaming

Ⓓ crying

15. How are Arliss and the bear cub similar?

Ⓐ They are good swimmers.

Ⓑ They are small for their age.

Ⓒ They can run fast.

Ⓓ They are too scared to think.

16. How does Old Yeller save Arliss?

Ⓐ He pulls Arliss away from the cub.

Ⓑ He attacks the mother bear.

Ⓒ He runs to get Travis.

Ⓓ He helps the cub get loose from Arliss.

17. How does Travis help Old Yeller save Arliss?

Ⓐ Travis pulls Arliss away from the cub.

Ⓑ Travis hits the mother bear with rocks.

Ⓒ Travis shoots the bear cub.

Ⓓ Travis attacks the mother bear with his axe.

Practice Book
Timeless Treasures

18. Who is the narrator in this selection?

Ⓐ Arliss

Ⓑ Mama

Ⓒ Travis

Ⓓ Old Yeller

19. The narrator says that Old Yeller ran straight at the mother bear, roaring like a mad bull. What does *roaring like a mad bull* mean?

_____

_____

_____

_____

_____

_____

_____

_____

_____

20. How does Travis feel about Arliss before the bear fight? after the bear fight?

_____

_____

_____

_____

_____

_____

_____

_____

© Harcourt

Trapped by the Ice!

Directions: For items 1–18, fill in the circle in front of the correct answer.
For items 19–20, write the answer.

Vocabulary

1. Since the sailors' supply of fresh water was gone, they would soon be suffering from _____ .

  Ⓐ optimism   Ⓑ dehydration

  Ⓒ craftiness   Ⓓ exhaustion

2. The butter sat out in the hot sun so long it turned _____ .

  Ⓐ creamy   Ⓑ rancid

  Ⓒ cooperative   Ⓓ effective

3. Because of the blizzard, the mountain gap was _____ .

  Ⓐ impassable   Ⓑ passable

  Ⓒ patriotic   Ⓓ hysterical

4. After the avalanche, the skiers spent ten _____ days stranded in the mountains before they were rescued.

  Ⓐ exasperated   Ⓑ grueling

  Ⓒ hysterical   Ⓓ abandoned

5. Have you ever _____ water from a boat?

  Ⓐ wailed   Ⓑ fumed

  Ⓒ waved   Ⓓ bailed

6. On the _____ journey across the mountains, the men were thankful no one was injured.

  Ⓐ leisurely   Ⓑ hilarious

  Ⓒ perilous   Ⓓ shrewd

Comprehension

7. This selection is mainly about _____ .
- Ⓐ the terrible ordeal Sir Shackleton and his men survived
- Ⓑ the sinking of the *Endurance* at the South Pole
- Ⓒ men exploring and discovering the South Pole
- Ⓓ camping out on Elephant Island

8. This true story happened about _____ .
- Ⓐ ten years ago
- Ⓑ 150 years ago
- Ⓒ 100 years ago
- Ⓓ 50 years ago

9. Sir Ernest Shackleton had set a goal to be the first person to _____ .
- Ⓐ reach the South Pole
- Ⓑ land on Elephant Island
- Ⓒ climb the North Pole's ice caps
- Ⓓ cross the South Pole's ice caps

10. In November, 1915, the *Endurance* _____ .
- Ⓐ was hit by an iceberg and cracked in half
- Ⓑ sank into and froze in the Weddell Sea
- Ⓒ was found by whalers and the crew saved
- Ⓓ was carried by ice to the open sea

11. The men mounted the lifeboats on sledges so _____ .
- Ⓐ the men could pull them across the ice
- Ⓑ horses could pull the sleds and save the men's strength
- Ⓒ they could reach the nearest land
- Ⓓ they could sail out in the Weddell Sea

12. When Tom was skiing back to camp, he _____ .
- Ⓐ was hunting penguins and seals
- Ⓑ tripped and broke his leg on the ice
- Ⓒ was attacked by a sea leopard
- Ⓓ caught a sea leopard

13. An ice floe is similar to an iceberg, but the ice floe is _____ .
- Ⓐ smaller but deeper
- Ⓑ the same thing
- Ⓒ larger and deeper
- Ⓓ a sheet-like piece of ice with not much depth

14. When sailing, the men kept from becoming dehydrated by _____ .
- Ⓐ drinking sea water
- Ⓑ sucking on frozen seal meat
- Ⓒ sucking on frozen sea leopard meat
- Ⓓ drinking fresh water

15. In April, Tom Crean tried to keep up the men's spirits _____ .
- Ⓐ by reading them letters from home
- Ⓑ but they were so discouraged nothing worked
- Ⓒ by singing and dancing for them
- Ⓓ by spotting South Georgia Island

16. When the men arrived at Elephant Island, their problems were not solved because the island _____ .
- Ⓐ had no telephone
- Ⓑ had no food or shelter
- Ⓒ had no people on it
- Ⓓ was nothing but a warm and windy rock

Practice Book
Timeless Treasures

17. Two men set up a temporary home in a cave on South Georgia Island because the men _____ .

   Ⓐ wanted to watch the sailing ships

   Ⓑ wanted to go whaling

   Ⓒ were too weak to hike across the island

   Ⓓ were able to get drinking water there

18. All of the following were major worries of the men staying on Elephant Island **except** _____ .

   Ⓐ building a permanent home on the island

   Ⓑ wondering if Shack was all right

   Ⓒ wondering if they would be rescued

   Ⓓ having too much food

19. Describe the men's last gamble and why it was successful.

_____

_____

_____

_____

_____

_____

20. How does Sir Ernest Shackleton's goal change from the beginning to the end of the selection?

_____

_____

_____

_____

_____

_____

Flood: Wrestling with the Mississippi

Directions: For items 1–18, fill in the circle in front of the correct answer. For items 19–20, write the answer.

Vocabulary

1. The most fertile farming soil is found in the _____ .
- Ⓐ floodwall
- Ⓑ atmosphere
- Ⓒ crevasse
- Ⓓ floodplain

2. The rain came _____ through the window and stained the wallpaper.
- Ⓐ lunging
- Ⓑ funding
- Ⓒ seeping
- Ⓓ glaring

3. The river rose so high that the _____ could no longer hold back the water.
- Ⓐ fences
- Ⓑ levees
- Ⓒ diamonds
- Ⓓ embarrassment

4. There has been so much rain this spring that the _____ are filled to capacity.
- Ⓐ reservoirs
- Ⓑ mountains
- Ⓒ optimism
- Ⓓ cascades

5. When the geyser erupted, we were _____ by the sheer force of the explosion.
- Ⓐ accepted
- Ⓑ lectured
- Ⓒ awed
- Ⓓ complied

Practice Book
Timeless Treasures

6. Sonia enjoyed visiting her grandparents, but she _____ to get back home among all her friends.

Ⓐ resisted   Ⓑ decreased

Ⓒ seasoned   Ⓓ yearned

7. During the recent floods in our area, the river _____ at eighteen feet.

Ⓐ rewrote   Ⓑ crested

Ⓒ complained   Ⓓ prescribed

Comprehension

8. Why did the Corps of Engineers build dams and reservoirs along the floodplain?

Ⓐ to flood land along the Mississippi

Ⓑ to keep water out of the main streets

Ⓒ to keep the Mississippi in its channel

Ⓓ to collect rainwater

9. In 1993 hot, moist air in the upper Midwest collided with cold air from Canada to cause _____ .

Ⓐ tornadoes

Ⓑ lots of rain

Ⓒ high temperatures

Ⓓ hot, dry air

10. In 1993 hot, dry air over the East Coast prevented the weather in the Midwest from _____ .

Ⓐ moving to the Gulf of Mexico

Ⓑ bringing more rain to the floodplain

Ⓒ heading west

Ⓓ breaking up and moving east

© Harcourt

11. So much rain had fallen by mid-July 1993 that _____ .
Ⓐ rivers flooded towns and farms in several states
Ⓑ the storms in the Midwest finally ended
Ⓒ weather scientists believed that the rain would soon stop
Ⓓ it was common for 5 to 12 inches of rain to fall in one hour

12. How was the one-mile section of the Sny Island levee rebuilt?
Ⓐ by pushing wet sand to the top of the levee
Ⓑ by building a wall of boards and supporting it with sandbags
Ⓒ by using wet earth to bulldoze the levees
Ⓓ by bringing sand from other states to make sandbags

13. What happened after part of the Sny levee gave way?
Ⓐ The rains began again.
Ⓑ People immediately rebuilt it.
Ⓒ Corn and soybeans stretched as far as the eye could see.
Ⓓ Thousands of acres of farmland lay under fifteen feet of water.

14. Prisoners helped the people of Niota, Illinois, by _____ .
Ⓐ being nice to the townspeople
Ⓑ not eating because the river flooded the town
Ⓒ working with them to place sandbags
Ⓓ crying when the levee broke

15. Davenport, Iowa, has no levees for all of the following reasons **except** _____ .
Ⓐ citizens didn't want to block their view of the river
Ⓑ citizens missed out on the chance to have the federal government build the levee
Ⓒ taxpayers didn't think they could afford to pay for the levee
Ⓓ citizens thought the flooding would wash the streets of the city

16. What saved Hannibal, Missouri, from the floodwaters?
Ⓐ Hannibal was the hometown of Mark Twain.
Ⓑ Its people had already raised the levee with sandbags.
Ⓒ Hannibal is not on a river.
Ⓓ The town is on a hill.

17. When could families return to their homes and farms?

(A) after the rains stopped

(B) after the Corps of Engineers built new levees

(C) after the floodwater drained back into the river

(D) before their livestock died

18. Why did the author write this selection?

(A) to explain the causes and effects of the 1993 flood

(B) to describe what causes rainy seasons

(C) to tell how farmlands get covered with water

(D) to explain how levees are built

19. Explain briefly why the Mississippi did not cause flooding south of Cape Girardeau and Cairo.

_____

_____

_____

_____

_____

_____

_____

_____

20. Why did people want to rebuild on the same land?

_____

_____

_____

_____

_____

_____

_____

Directions: For items 1–18, fill in the circle in front of the correct answer. For items 19–20, write the answer.

Vocabulary

1. After the storm, the farmer inspected his fields, _____ the rows for any signs of plants that might be saved.
   - Ⓐ raising
   - Ⓑ scouring
   - Ⓒ researching
   - Ⓓ freshening

2. We always trade at this store because the owner is a _____ supplier of fresh, clean fruits and vegetables.
   - Ⓐ reliable
   - Ⓑ renovated
   - Ⓒ defiant
   - Ⓓ starving

3. The restaurant's _____ is a rich chocolate dessert served with a hot sauce.
   - Ⓐ species
   - Ⓑ burden
   - Ⓒ specialty
   - Ⓓ assembly

4. The cactus and other plants not requiring much water _____ in the arid desert.
   - Ⓐ nourished
   - Ⓑ isolated
   - Ⓒ solved
   - Ⓓ flourished

5. Some people think a computer is nothing but a _____ gadget that is difficult to use.
   - Ⓐ grueling
   - Ⓑ newfangled
   - Ⓒ shiny
   - Ⓓ clumsy

6. Our new neighbors seem to be very _____ and a nice addition to the neighborhood.
   - Ⓐ crafty
   - Ⓑ sociable
   - Ⓒ rowdy
   - Ⓓ imperious

7. The campers found that the meat cooks better over the open fire if they _____ it first.

(A) skewer

(B) issue

(C) peck

(D) isolate

8. Everyone was _____ by the number of volunteers who arrived to work at the school fair.

(A) uniformed

(B) tousled

(C) astounded

(D) abandoned

Comprehension

9. Icecaps cause problems such as _____ .

(A) too much rain

(B) too many animals having to move near the water

(C) animals and people having to move to warmer places

(D) the oceans growing

10. In this selection, why is the Russian family moving south?

(A) to find better hunting

(B) to get away from snow

(C) to explore a new area

(D) to find better skiing

11. According to the selection, in 8400 B.C. people in the Middle East tried to _____ .

(A) stay close to the river

(B) move away from the river

(C) farm

(D) hunt

12. Why are people in Syria experimenting with seeds?
(A) They want flower gardens.
(B) They are trying to grow their own food.
(C) They have had an extra amount of rain.
(D) Gardening is hard work.

13. Why do hunters decide they want tame wolves?
(A) The wolves are good with children.
(B) Wolves try to smile.
(C) Wolves can climb trees to follow hunted animals.
(D) The wolves can find hidden animals.

14. According to the selection, roasted meat is tasty, and _____ .
(A) families enjoy being together around the fire
(B) family members take turns eating
(C) it is easy to make in any oven
(D) people get different things to eat every day

15. One way to make a tepee water-resistant, according to the selection, is to _____ .
(A) rub the skins with animal fat
(B) use very thick skins
(C) choose a sheltered, well-drained site
(D) place all the tepees in a circle

16. "The Stone Age News" states that vessels are first made by the _____ .
(A) experimenter
(B) farmers of Syria
(C) Joman people of Japan
(D) deer hunters

17. What benefit does pottery bring to the Stone Age?
(A) Making pottery is a new way of using clay.
(B) Making pottery has taught people how to control the size of fires.
(C) People can now eat fish.
(D) Pottery can be used for cooking.

18. Why did the author write the selection in this way?

Ⓐ to introduce the reader to real people from the Stone Age

Ⓑ to tell facts about the Stone Age in an entertaining way

Ⓒ to make fun of people who are different

Ⓓ to tell information about the Stone Age

19. Learning how to grow crops is important to the development of villages because

_____

_____

_____

_____

_____

_____

_____

20. How are the boil-in-bag method of cooking and using pottery for cooking similar?

_____

_____

_____

_____

_____

_____

_____

_____

_____

Practice Book
Timeless Treasures

Ancient China

Directions: For items 1–18, fill in the circle in front of the correct answer.
For items 19–20, write the answer.

Vocabulary

1. Most of the country's crops failed during the drought, resulting in
widespread _____ .
- Ⓐ possession
- Ⓑ famine
- Ⓒ appeal
- Ⓓ victory

2. The dancers' costumes were quite _____, with hundreds of hand-stitched
beads forming complex patterns.
- Ⓐ jealous
- Ⓑ mortal
- Ⓒ elaborate
- Ⓓ exhausted

3. The king invited all the _____ of his kingdom to attend a royal parade.
- Ⓐ articles
- Ⓑ assurances
- Ⓒ initials
- Ⓓ inhabitants

4. The Chinese _____ is one of the oldest cultures in the known world.
- Ⓐ ordinance
- Ⓑ civilization
- Ⓒ memento
- Ⓓ district

5. Since my mother received her promotion, she finds she is doing
more _____ work.
- Ⓐ administrative
- Ⓑ occupational
- Ⓒ unaccompanied
- Ⓓ hysterical

6. Because the countryside is so hilly, the best way to grow crops is with a
system of _____ .
- Ⓐ porches
- Ⓑ peasants
- Ⓒ terraces
- Ⓓ estates

Comprehension

7. According to this selection, a _____ is considered to be a family that has ruled in a country for a long period of time.

   Ⓐ monarch

   Ⓑ dynasty

   Ⓒ emperor

   Ⓓ landlord

8. Why did the Chinese civilization begin around the Yellow River?

   Ⓐ There was plenty of water in the area.

   Ⓑ It was a holy place.

   Ⓒ The area had good farmland.

   Ⓓ It was the first place the settlers looked.

9. What are rice paddies?

   Ⓐ places where rice is grown

   Ⓑ something good to eat

   Ⓒ stores that sell rice

   Ⓓ special soil in the rice fields

10. Why did the emperor build the Great Wall of China?

   Ⓐ to provide a place to exercise

   Ⓑ to protect China from its enemies

   Ⓒ to keep his army busy

   Ⓓ to experiment with a new building technique

11. What is one thing that is unusual about the laws in the Forbidden City?

   Ⓐ The Forbidden City allows no human being inside it.

   Ⓑ The emperor is the only male allowed in the Forbidden City after dark.

   Ⓒ Government workers are allowed inside the city at night.

   Ⓓ Money couldn't pass hands in the Forbidden City.

12. Where is the walled imperial city?
- Ⓐ in Beijing
- Ⓑ in the Forbidden City
- Ⓒ in Tibet
- Ⓓ on the Great Wall

13. Why was the road to the Forbidden City made long and straight?
- Ⓐ Guards could see anyone approaching from a distance.
- Ⓑ Long roads made the palace look more important.
- Ⓒ It was easier to build a straight road.
- Ⓓ It was the law in China that roads must be straight.

14. In a government that has a civil service system, people get government jobs by _____ .
- Ⓐ having friends who work in the government
- Ⓑ being part of the army
- Ⓒ taking and passing exams
- Ⓓ having relatives who work in the government

15. According to this selection, the dragon represents _____ to the Chinese.
- Ⓐ hard work
- Ⓑ fun and excitement
- Ⓒ sadness and turmoil
- Ⓓ joy and happiness

16. The earliest Chinese writing was done on _____ .
- Ⓐ paper
- Ⓑ bamboo
- Ⓒ animal bones
- Ⓓ silk

17. Why was the invention of printing important?
- Ⓐ It was much faster than copying books by hand.
- Ⓑ It used paper, which was the cheapest writing material.
- Ⓒ It was easy to carve characters into wood.
- Ⓓ Printed copies were hard to make.

Practice Book
Timeless Treasures

18. According to the selection, which pair of objects was invented by the Chinese?

(A) the compass and jade

(B) the lawn mower and the compass

(C) rice and paper

(D) the wheelbarrow and the clock

19. In Chinese cities, how were the homes of the poor and the rich different?

_____

_____

_____

_____

_____

_____

_____

_____

_____

20. How is Chinese writing different from English writing?

_____

_____

_____

_____

_____

_____

_____

_____

_____

_____

Pyramids

Directions: For items 1–18, fill in the circle in front of the correct answer. For items 19–20, write the answer.

Vocabulary

1. The old castle had two secret _____ that led outside to the gardens.
   - Ⓐ permissions
   - Ⓑ collections
   - Ⓒ coins
   - Ⓓ passageways

2. The accountant developed an _____ method of recording checks that should make our bookkeeping faster and easier.
   - Ⓐ ingenious
   - Ⓑ insufficient
   - Ⓒ offensive
   - Ⓓ elastic

3. The cabin was in an _____ location with no neighbors for miles around.
   - Ⓐ unfolded
   - Ⓒ isolated
   - Ⓑ ejected
   - Ⓓ inflicted

4. During the summer an _____ from the university is taking students to Italy to dig for ancient treasures.
   - Ⓐ attempt
   - Ⓒ archaeologist
   - Ⓑ empire
   - Ⓓ editor

5. The marble used for the floors in the new courthouse was mined from several _____ .
   - Ⓐ valleys
   - Ⓒ levees
   - Ⓑ hovels
   - Ⓓ quarries

6. Archaeologists have learned much about life in ancient times by studying objects that have been _____ .
   - Ⓐ preserved
   - Ⓒ astounded
   - Ⓑ pressured
   - Ⓓ exhausted

Comprehension

7. The selection mentions the Seven Wonders of the Ancient World. Which is still standing?

Ⓐ the Eiffel Tower

Ⓑ the Statue of Liberty

Ⓒ the Leaning Tower of Pisa

Ⓓ the Pyramids of Giza

8. The pyramids were built to _____ .

Ⓐ provide work for ancient Egyptians

Ⓑ be tombs for the pharaohs

Ⓒ provide places for pharaohs to explore

Ⓓ reflect the desert sunlight

9. In the selection, what does the phrase *circle of isolation* refer to?

Ⓐ Egypt is shaped like a circle.

Ⓑ Egyptians like to be alone.

Ⓒ Geographic features protect Egypt on all sides.

Ⓓ Enemies surround Egypt.

10. Since 1970, the Nile has not flooded the farmlands in the summer because _____ .

Ⓐ the river has dried up

Ⓑ a new levee system was installed

Ⓒ the Aswan Dam was built

Ⓓ the summers have had no rain

11. Why was limestone used to build most pyramids?

Ⓐ Egypt has a lot of limestone.

Ⓑ Limestone is close to the building sites.

Ⓒ It is not expensive.

Ⓓ It is very lightweight.

© Harcourt

12. The location of the pyramids was determined by _____ .

Ⓐ military reasons

Ⓑ religious and practical reasons

Ⓒ unknown reasons

Ⓓ the Egyptian climate

13. Why did builders include false passages and fake burial chambers in the pyramids?

Ⓐ to make the pyramids larger

Ⓑ to provide escape routes for workers

Ⓒ to impress visitors

Ⓓ to keep the treasures inside safe from robbers

14. How do we know that the builders wanted to make sure that workers could breathe while inside a pyramid?

Ⓐ by the giant fans that have been found

Ⓑ from the air shafts that were built

Ⓒ from the building plans that were found

Ⓓ from notes that the kings wrote about it

15. What was the reason for mummification?

Ⓐ to protect the body from animals

Ⓑ to make something beautiful

Ⓒ to keep the body in good condition for the next life

Ⓓ to take care of dental problems

16. Scientists have found mummies of people and of _____ .

Ⓐ cats and crocodiles

Ⓑ plants and weeds

Ⓒ horses and cows

Ⓓ spiders and butterflies

Practice Book
Timeless Treasures

17. Pharaoh Khafre built the Sphinx _____ .

   Ⓐ instead of a pyramid for his final resting place

   Ⓑ with king's and queen's chambers

   Ⓒ with a lion's face and his body

   Ⓓ to guard his pyramid

18. How was King Tut's tomb different from all the others in the Valley of the Kings?

   Ⓐ It had not been robbed of all its treasures.

   Ⓑ It never had treasures in it.

   Ⓒ It was not sealed.

   Ⓓ It was never found.

19. List two things that people have learned from the pyramids.

_____

_____

_____

_____

_____

_____

20. How are pyramids all over the world similar in construction?

_____

_____

_____

_____

_____

_____

Look Into the Past: The Greeks and the Romans

Directions: For items 1–18, fill in the circle in front of the correct answer. For items 19–20, write the answer.

Vocabulary

1. In art class we are making a _____ that shows a historical scene.
   - (A) diagnosis
   - (B) mosaic
   - (C) rhythm
   - (D) fraction

2. The school nurse spoke to us about why good _____ is important to our health.
   - (A) hygiene
   - (B) escalation
   - (C) plunder
   - (D) antagonism

3. Have you seen the _____ John designed for our new band uniforms?
   - (A) waver
   - (B) cinder
   - (C) emblem
   - (D) aqueduct

4. In ancient times, water was brought from the river to the town through an _____.
   - (A) alphabet
   - (B) archaeologist
   - (C) estate
   - (D) aqueduct

5. When a fire destroyed most of the house, it was necessary to _____ the kitchen.
   - (A) reconstruct
   - (B) quench
   - (C) condense
   - (D) produce

6. The United States is divided into states, but Canada is divided into _____.
   - (A) countries
   - (B) estates
   - (C) provinces
   - (D) intervals

Comprehension

7. Many people consider that the greatest period of Greek civilization was _____ .
   - (A) 100 years ago
   - (B) 1,000 years ago
   - (C) 2,500 years ago
   - (D) 3,500 years ago

8. The ancient Greek alphabet and the English alphabet are _____ .
   - (A) completely different
   - (B) exactly the same
   - (C) very similar
   - (D) based on the Egyptian alphabet

9. Why were women in Athens generally not able to read or write?
   - (A) Girls did not go to school.
   - (B) Girls weren't interested in school.
   - (C) Girls had no transportation to school.
   - (D) There were no schools in Athens.

10. Athens was a rich and powerful city-state because _____ .
    - (A) Athena was the patron goddess of Athens
    - (B) slaves mined silver from the mine just outside the city
    - (C) Pericles was a wise ruler of Athens
    - (D) an owl was the emblem for the city-state

11. Who could vote in ancient Athens?
    - (A) free-born males
    - (B) all adults
    - (C) free adults and freed slaves
    - (D) all men

Name _____ Date _____

12. How do we know that indoor running water is not a new invention?
- (A) There has always been indoor running water.
- (B) A queen ordered that someone find a way to do it 1,000 years ago.
- (C) Ancient Greek houses had indoor running water.
- (D) It was used in a palace on Crete 3,500 years ago.

13. The Greeks planned their temples by using the study of _____ .
- (A) literature
- (B) music
- (C) mathematics
- (D) physical education

14. In a Greek play, the chorus helped the audience to _____ .
- (A) hear the actors better
- (B) understand the play better
- (C) take part in the play itself
- (D) learn the songs to sing along

15. The Roman Empire was linked by an impressive network of roads. In this selection, *network* refers to _____ .
- (A) a system in which the parts are connected
- (B) an exchange of information between individuals or groups
- (C) a radio or television company that produces programs
- (D) wires that cross and are knotted at the crossings

16. All the following took place at the forum **except** _____ .
- (A) listening to speeches
- (B) participating in city council meetings
- (C) trading goods
- (D) training of troops

Practice Book
Timeless Treasures

17. What was Rome like in A.D. 100?

    Ⓐ It was just starting to grow.

    Ⓑ It was the largest city in the world.

    Ⓒ It had a few thousand people.

    Ⓓ It was a very poor city.

18. The Roman language is called "Latin" because _____ .

    Ⓐ the original settlers were the Latini tribe

    Ⓑ the Latini tribe were educated people and created the language

    Ⓒ Latium is north of the Greek settlements

    Ⓓ the Roman army named the language

19. List two things that let us know that the Romans were concerned with health and hygiene.

_____

_____

_____

_____

_____

_____

_____

20. What is the present-day importance of Pompeii and Herculaneum?

_____

_____

_____

_____

_____

_____

_____

_____

© Harcourt

The Skill of Pericles

Directions: For items 1–18, fill in the circle in front of the correct answer. For items 19–20, write the answer.

Vocabulary

1. It was difficult to _____ him from his deep sleep.
   - Ⓐ mature
   - Ⓑ imply
   - Ⓒ rouse
   - Ⓓ depend

2. The celebrity _____ himself so that he could walk through the crowds without being recognized.
   - Ⓐ dominated
   - Ⓑ disguised
   - Ⓒ consisted
   - Ⓓ collapsed

3. Patience and honesty are just two of her many _____ .
   - Ⓐ violins
   - Ⓑ virtues
   - Ⓒ insults
   - Ⓓ echoes

4. During the awful storm at sea, the only way the captain could communicate orders to the crew was by _____ them.
   - Ⓐ bellowing
   - Ⓑ whispering
   - Ⓒ lunging
   - Ⓓ charging

5. Since we live in a _____ society, we have a voice in the laws of the land.
   - Ⓐ dominated
   - Ⓑ commercial
   - Ⓒ professional
   - Ⓓ democratic

6. Once the fighting started even the gentlest of people turned into _____ .

Ⓐ chariots

Ⓑ geologists

Ⓒ brutes

Ⓓ peasants

Comprehension

7. The setting and time of this play is _____ .

Ⓐ a modern-day Athens market place

Ⓑ Athens in the fifth century A.D.

Ⓒ a Sparta market place in the fifth century B.C.

Ⓓ an Athens market place in the fifth century B.C.

8. Cimon is considered to be the best _____ in Athens.

Ⓐ warrior

Ⓑ athlete

Ⓒ friend

Ⓓ orator

9. When the play begins, the Old Sailor is _____ .

Ⓐ disguised as Pericles

Ⓑ reading from a book

Ⓒ talking with his friend Pericles

Ⓓ telling a story to young people

10. The Old Sailor is telling the young people about the Cyclops, who _____ .

Ⓐ has one eye in the middle of his forehead

Ⓑ has a gift for telling wonderful stories

Ⓒ is very handsome

Ⓓ owns a large fleet of ships

© Harcourt

11. Who is Pericles?
- (A) a friend of the Old Sailor
- (B) the leader of Athens
- (C) a messenger
- (D) a companion of Odysseus

12. According to the messenger, why is Pericles visiting?
- (A) He is spying on the citizens of Athens.
- (B) He is looking for a youth who best knows the skill of Pericles.
- (C) He is learning how to dance and sing.
- (D) He is planning to hold an important government meeting.

13. After the messenger reads his announcement, what do some of the citizens discuss?
- (A) what the prize may be
- (B) how Odysseus beats the Cyclops
- (C) whose children can win the prize
- (D) where the Old Sailor has gone

14. As the citizens talk, what is Pericles doing?
- (A) talking to the Old Sailor
- (B) running a foot race with Cimon
- (C) looking for his messenger
- (D) pretending to be a half-asleep beggar

15. How do most of the young people feel about the challenge from Pericles?
- (A) excited about possibly winning the prize
- (B) not worthy of winning
- (C) scared of the challenge
- (D) angry that Pericles has interrupted their story

16. How does Pericles treat all the young people?
- (A) He acts as if he doesn't like any of them.
- (B) He is in a great hurry and has no time to talk.
- (C) He doesn't want to hear any of their opinions.
- (D) He listens to them and respects their ideas.

17. How does Pericles decide who will win the prize?

Ⓐ by letting the people choose

Ⓑ by asking the Old Sailor's opinion

Ⓒ by asking only the young people

Ⓓ by choosing Nestor

18. What is the real reason Pericles visits the people?

Ⓐ to take up some of his spare time

Ⓑ to teach them about democracy

Ⓒ to visit with his friend the Old Sailor

Ⓓ to find more soldiers for his army

19. Why doesn't Pericles make his identity known at first?

_____

_____

_____

_____

_____

_____

_____

20. During the play, different people represent skills and qualities that the ancient Greeks admire. Name three of these skills and qualities.

_____

_____

_____

_____

_____

_____

_____

My Side of the Mountain

Directions: For items 1–18, fill in the circle in front of the correct answer. For items 19–20, write the answer.

Vocabulary

1. It is time for the birds' annual _____ to warmer climates.
- Ⓐ inquiry
- Ⓑ migration
- Ⓒ molting
- Ⓓ solution

2. There were cracks in the _____ of the old house, and repairing them would be costly.
- Ⓐ foundation
- Ⓑ function
- Ⓒ abolition
- Ⓓ elimination

3. It was _____ to see that our canoe was filling with water faster than we could bail it out.
- Ⓐ disapproving
- Ⓑ disallowing
- Ⓒ discouraging
- Ⓓ disbarring

4. Are these plants _____, or will it make us sick to eat them?
- Ⓐ thankful
- Ⓑ edible
- Ⓒ emotional
- Ⓓ honorable

5. The campers set up camp in a _____ section of the island far away from other campers.
- Ⓐ disguised
- Ⓑ reconstructed
- Ⓒ tremulous
- Ⓓ remote

6. The fruits and nuts provided a _____ snack after our long walk.
- Ⓐ specialty
- Ⓑ newfangled
- Ⓒ nourishing
- Ⓓ unwavering

7. The woodpeckers drilled a hole in the tree, and then they made a nest in the _____ .
- Ⓐ cavity
- Ⓑ loam
- Ⓒ hovel
- Ⓓ wedges

Comprehension

8. What does the narrator collect from a stream to eat?
- Ⓐ almost a peck of mussels
- Ⓑ a bucket of clams
- Ⓒ handfuls of hickory nuts
- Ⓓ some apples and walnuts

9. According to the selection, why does the narrator study the animals' behavior?
- Ⓐ It is possible to predict storms from animal actions.
- Ⓑ Whatever the animals eat is safe for humans to eat.
- Ⓒ The narrator wants to be a biologist when he grows up.
- Ⓓ Animal behavior can reveal if people are approaching.

10. What does the narrator do as he discovers parts of the property?
- Ⓐ makes notes on scraps of paper
- Ⓑ puts *x*'s on a map
- Ⓒ takes pictures
- Ⓓ tape-records what he notices

11. Why does the narrator want a home that is not visible to others?
- Ⓐ He does not like people who hunt or camp.
- Ⓑ He likes his privacy.
- Ⓒ He is afraid he will not be allowed to stay if he is found living alone.
- Ⓓ He wants to become part of the wilderness.

12. How does the narrator make a home?
- Ⓐ He cuts and burns away part of a tree.
- Ⓑ He finds a cave.
- Ⓒ He makes a home behind some boulders.
- Ⓓ He puts up a tent.

13. What does the narrator find for his dinner?
- Ⓐ beetles
- Ⓑ arrow-leaf
- Ⓒ crayfish
- Ⓓ cattails

14. At first, what does the narrator think that he can use to put out the fire?

Ⓐ the wet boulders

Ⓑ water from the rushing stream

Ⓒ water from the lake

Ⓓ water from the bathtub-sized spring

15. "How can I get water back to the tree? That's how citified I was in those days." In this selection, *citified* means _____ .

Ⓐ has a certificate

Ⓑ is used to city ways

Ⓒ doesn't like the city

Ⓓ frequently goes to a city

16. What does the narrator finally realize he can use instead of water to put out the fire?

Ⓐ a sweater

Ⓑ a pail of mussels

Ⓒ a handful of dirt

Ⓓ a handful of leaves

17. Who is the narrator of this selection?

Ⓐ a boy from New York city

Ⓑ a hunter

Ⓒ a farmer

Ⓓ Miss Turner

18. If you wanted to borrow this book from a library, in which section would you be most likely to find it?

Ⓐ realistic fiction

Ⓑ mystery

Ⓒ science fiction

Ⓓ autobiographical

19. What does the narrator do that makes him feel pleased with himself?

_____

_____

_____

_____

_____

_____

_____

_____

_____

20. How does the narrator keep track of time?

_____

_____

_____

_____

_____

_____

_____

_____

_____

Practice Book
Timeless Treasures

Directions: For items 1–18, fill in the circle in front of the correct answer. For items 19–20, write the answer.

Vocabulary

1. Despite many disappointments, Sarah _____ and kept on following her dreams.

   Ⓐ ceased   Ⓑ persevered

   Ⓒ chattered   Ⓓ tightened

2. I want to see the _____ of the first-place trophy to the winner.

   Ⓐ pardon   Ⓑ pattern

   Ⓒ motion   Ⓓ presentation

3. The jewel had no faults or blemishes; it was absolutely _____ .

   Ⓐ humorless   Ⓑ bored

   Ⓒ flawless   Ⓓ discarded

4. The early settlers in this country provided us the great _____ of freedom.

   Ⓐ legacy   Ⓑ console

   Ⓒ recording   Ⓓ ordinance

5. The _____ piano filled the hall with music, so we all decided to sing along.

   Ⓐ elaborate   Ⓑ democratic

   Ⓒ recital   Ⓓ melodious

6. The girls sang the cheerful song with clear _____ voices.

   Ⓐ rancid   Ⓑ sad

   Ⓒ lilting   Ⓓ awed

Comprehension

7. What is one probable reason the girls did not do as well as they expected to in the audition?

Ⓐ They hadn't practiced enough.

Ⓑ They made too many mistakes.

Ⓒ The competition is tough.

Ⓓ They forgot to wear good-luck charms.

8. What is one of Jessie's first thoughts after she reads the audition results?

Ⓐ She thinks that she must have "blown it."

Ⓑ She thinks that she is a failure.

Ⓒ She wants to find her three friends.

Ⓓ She doesn't want the role she received.

9. Instead of getting the part of Harriet Tubman as an old woman, Jessie gets the role of _____ .

Ⓐ Harriet as a young girl

Ⓑ Harriet's sister

Ⓒ Harriet's mother

Ⓓ Harriet's second husband

10. After reading the audition results, Jessie and Mkiwa worry mostly about _____ .

Ⓐ disappointing their families

Ⓑ looking foolish to their friends

Ⓒ not being together in the play

Ⓓ auditioning again

11. How does Julie feel about the audition results compared to the way Jessie and Mkiwa feel?

Ⓐ She isn't as talented as the others.

Ⓑ She doesn't have any family to disappoint.

Ⓒ She knows she hasn't practiced that much.

Ⓓ She has more reasonable expectations for herself.

12. What does Julie teach the other three about being professional?

(A) Professionals are the best kind of artists.

(B) Professionals do their best all the time.

(C) Professionals learn from their mistakes.

(D) Professionals know how to have fun.

13. Why does Jessie call herself and her three friends "Dreamgirls"?

(A) They all daydream about their futures.

(B) They all are beautiful and charming.

(C) They all have special dreams and talents.

(D) All their dreams have come true.

14. Why did Maria's father not support her desire to become a concert pianist at first?

(A) He felt she might have trouble being accepted as a Mexican female concert pianist.

(B) He thought Maria wasn't talented enough to be a concert pianist.

(C) The family can't afford to buy Maria a piano for practice.

(D) He felt Maria wouldn't make much money as a concert pianist.

15. Why do the girls feel better about their talents after they perform at Evergreen?

(A) They haven't made any mistakes.

(B) Their families are there to support them.

(C) They know they are going to get a good grade.

(D) The audience appreciates their talents.

16. "Julie persevered in the face of enormous hardships" means that she _____ .

(A) decided to quit when it got tough

(B) selected the oldest and hardest instrument to play

(C) didn't give up even though she had to overcome difficulties

(D) is happy when she is playing the violin

Practice Book
Timeless Treasures

17. Jessie is nervous when it is her turn to perform at Evergreen because _____ .

Ⓐ she doesn't want to disappoint the audience

Ⓑ the other girls are depending on her

Ⓒ her family is in the audience

Ⓓ the other girls have performed perfectly

18. Each of the Dreamgirls has a different talent, but the one thing they have in common is _____ .

Ⓐ the desire to be actresses

Ⓑ the desire and drive to succeed

Ⓒ to not practice on a regular basis

Ⓓ to sing at the retirement home

19. According to the story, what personal qualities, besides talent, are needed for success?

_____

_____

_____

_____

_____

20. Why does each girl continue to pursue her art despite disappointments?

_____

_____

_____

_____

_____

_____

Directions: For items 1–18, fill in the circle in front of the correct answer. For items 19–20, write the answer.

Vocabulary

1. Through creativity and _____ Gina designed a workable invention.
   (A) province
   (B) persistence
   (C) persuasion
   (D) compliments

2. The principal _____ all the students with perfect attendance at the assembly.
   (A) disguised
   (B) implemented
   (C) acknowledged
   (D) persevered

3. After several _____ about the science topic, the librarian posted some Internet sources for the students to research.
   (A) inquiries
   (B) quarries
   (C) emblems
   (D) rouses

4. To honor a great _____ in our grandparents' lives, we gave a party to celebrate their sixtieth wedding anniversary.
   (A) mosaic
   (B) foundation
   (C) milestone
   (D) occupation

5. The _____ rehearsal of the play proved that additional practice was needed before the actors were ready to perform for an audience.
   (A) favored
   (B) resourceful
   (C) flawless
   (D) initial

6. The inventor used a great deal of _____ in creating his invention.
   (A) specialty
   (B) legacy
   (C) ingenuity
   (D) anguish

7. To improve the _____ in the newly designed cars, the engineers added a larger rearview window to the design.
   (A) visibility
   (B) stability
   (C) motion
   (D) speed

Comprehension

8. This selection is mostly about _____ .
- Ⓐ women who become millionaires
- Ⓑ ingenious inventions of the past
- Ⓒ ingenious inventions by women
- Ⓓ men's milestones in history

9. Madam C. J. Walker, the first black woman to earn a million dollars on her own, invented _____ .
- Ⓐ hats for men
- Ⓑ hair-care products
- Ⓒ laundry soap
- Ⓓ creativity

10. Mary Anderson's invention was practical, but ahead of its time because _____ .
- Ⓐ no one thought it would sell
- Ⓑ she let her patent expire
- Ⓒ windshield wipers are only needed in bad weather
- Ⓓ no one thought windshield wipers were practical

11. Before windshield wipers were available, drivers _____ to improve visibility.
- Ⓐ drove very fast in the rain
- Ⓑ created a film with oil on the windshield
- Ⓒ created a film on the windshield with carrots and onions
- Ⓓ stuck their heads out the side window

12. Initially, flat-bottomed paper bags were very expensive because _____ .
- Ⓐ no one would buy them
- Ⓑ they had to be made by hand
- Ⓒ Margaret Knight changed the paper bag industry
- Ⓓ people liked to put groceries in wooden crates

13. Margaret Knight was nicknamed "Lady Edison" because _____ .
Ⓐ like Edison, she invented three things
Ⓑ she was Edison's wife
Ⓒ she became a mechanical engineer
Ⓓ like Edison, she applied for many patents

14. Why has the Glo-sheet proved to be so successful?
Ⓐ Becky and her father are good sales people.
Ⓑ There was a big need for the product.
Ⓒ Becky experimented with phosphorescent paint.
Ⓓ Becky is very ingenious.

15. NASA was curious about Becky's Glo-sheets because _____ .
Ⓐ she is a child
Ⓑ if she had been a former employee, they would own the patent
Ⓒ they thought she stole the idea from them
Ⓓ she is the youngest female to receive a patent

16. A legal document issued by the government to protect an idea is _____ .
Ⓐ a diagram   Ⓑ a trademark
Ⓒ a patent   Ⓓ an invention

17. To apply for a patent you must use a patent _____ .
Ⓐ teacher or principal
Ⓑ attorney or agent
Ⓒ owner or inventor
Ⓓ official of the government

18. All the inventions mentioned in this selection have the following in common **except** that they _____ .
Ⓐ were invented by men
Ⓑ fill a need people have
Ⓒ make life easier
Ⓓ were invented by women

19. What is the difference between a utility patent and a design patent?

_____

_____

_____

_____

_____

_____

_____

_____

_____

20. List at least two uses for Becky Schroeder's Glo-sheets.

_____

_____

_____

_____

_____

_____

_____

_____

_____

_____

Directions: For items 1–18, fill in the circle in front of the correct answer. For items 19–20, write the answer.

Vocabulary

1. Each bar on the graph will _____ a different country.
   - Ⓐ represent
   - Ⓑ return
   - Ⓒ resist
   - Ⓓ revolt

2. A parasite is _____ on its host organism for food.
   - Ⓐ requested
   - Ⓑ dependent
   - Ⓒ partial
   - Ⓓ exasperated

3. The painting was so _____ that the people in it appeared to be alive.
   - Ⓐ realistic
   - Ⓑ immature
   - Ⓒ reduced
   - Ⓓ artificial

4. When he retired, my uncle received a gold watch in _____ of his years of service with the company.
   - Ⓐ retaliation
   - Ⓑ recognition
   - Ⓒ superstition
   - Ⓓ saturation

5. Since a box has height, width, and length, it is _____ .
   - Ⓐ newfangled
   - Ⓑ flourishing
   - Ⓒ commercial
   - Ⓓ three-dimensional

6. For her birthday, Mother received a _____ glass animal to add to her collection.
   - Ⓐ milestone
   - Ⓑ miniature
   - Ⓒ skewer
   - Ⓓ cascade

Comprehension

7. This story is most like realistic fiction because _____ .
- Ⓐ the event could really happen
- Ⓑ the story takes place a long time ago
- Ⓒ the story explains "why" something in nature happened
- Ⓓ the story is written in rhyme

8. "I have to make a diorama for my Natural Science class." In this selection, a *diorama* is _____ .
- Ⓐ a box of cellophane and painted walls
- Ⓑ a science contest
- Ⓒ some painted objects
- Ⓓ a miniature scene in a box

9. How does Mrs. Frank help Mari?
- Ⓐ She shows Mari pictures of projects and finds books for her.
- Ⓑ She helps Mari get boxes and materials.
- Ⓒ She tells Mari what the other students are doing.
- Ⓓ She gives Mari some models to use in the project.

10. What does Mari first ask her mother to do for the project?
- Ⓐ to get some boxes and give her money
- Ⓑ to buy some paints at the store
- Ⓒ to call Papa and ask him for money
- Ⓓ to help her make the diorama

11. What is Mari's main problem throughout the actual making of the project?
- Ⓐ She cannot find boxes.
- Ⓑ She does not have money for supplies.
- Ⓒ She wants her parents to help her.
- Ⓓ She does not know how to do the project.

12. How does Mari solve her problem?
- Ⓐ by asking the librarian for help
- Ⓑ by asking her father for money and supplies
- Ⓒ by finding some materials and making objects
- Ⓓ by deciding she can't win anyway

13. How does Mari's mother help her with the project?
- Ⓐ by listening to her talk about the project
- Ⓑ by making suggestions for what to do
- Ⓒ by taking her to the beach to look for things
- Ⓓ by buying her paint, glitter, and fish

14. To make modeling clay for her creatures, Mari uses all of the following **except** _____ .
- Ⓐ flour
- Ⓑ salt
- Ⓒ sugar
- Ⓓ water

15. Why does Mari feel sad when she hears the other students talking about their projects?
- Ⓐ They are smarter than she is.
- Ⓑ Their parents are helping them.
- Ⓒ They are going to win the awards.
- Ⓓ They are having more fun with the project than she is.

16. When Mari talks to Mrs. Frank about her project, the librarian is _____ .
- Ⓐ angry
- Ⓑ suspicious
- Ⓒ doubtful
- Ⓓ enthusiastic

17. Why does Mari think that her project will not impress the other students?
- Ⓐ Some projects show that parents helped.
- Ⓑ Mari's project does not have museum fish.
- Ⓒ Her project does not have the finished look of store-bought materials.
- Ⓓ All of her materials are store-bought.

Practice Book
Timeless Treasures

18. Why is Mari glad that the projects are displayed in the library?

Ⓐ She doesn't want classmates to make fun of her project.

Ⓑ She wants Mrs. Frank to see her project.

Ⓒ She thinks that she may win if the projects are judged there.

Ⓓ Mrs. Frank will take a picture of her project.

19. How does Mari feel as the judges start handing out prizes? after she wins first prize?

_____

_____

_____

_____

_____

_____

_____

_____

20. Why does Mari say that Mamá gave her the best help that anyone could?

_____

_____

_____

_____

_____

_____

_____

_____

_____

Catching the Fire: Philip Simmons, Blacksmith

Directions: For items 1–18, fill in the circle in front of the correct answer. For items 19–20, write the answer.

Vocabulary

1. In the center of the garden stand two large _____ sculptures.
   - Ⓐ omitted
   - Ⓑ ornamental
   - Ⓒ envious
   - Ⓓ grateful

2. Will you help me _____ this new lock on my door?
   - Ⓐ exercise
   - Ⓑ humiliate
   - Ⓒ install
   - Ⓓ imitate

3. This _____ fan is helpful in the summer because it can be carried from room to room.
   - Ⓐ patient
   - Ⓑ portable
   - Ⓒ anxious
   - Ⓓ refused

4. The famous poet received many _____ honoring him for his work.
   - Ⓐ tributes
   - Ⓑ trespassers
   - Ⓒ dismissals
   - Ⓓ contests

5. After a long summer of working on road construction, the college boys had grown _____ and muscular.
   - Ⓐ remote
   - Ⓑ shrewd
   - Ⓒ stern
   - Ⓓ rugged

6. The blacksmith heated the horseshoe on the _____ so he could make a new shoe for the horse.
   - Ⓐ gorge
   - Ⓑ peak
   - Ⓒ forge
   - Ⓓ memento

Comprehension

7. Why was Philip Simmons well known in his time?
- (A) He was an African American.
- (B) He knew the traditional ways of working iron.
- (C) He liked to teach young people.
- (D) He made ship parts for the Navy.

8. Why was John Vlach impressed with Philip Simmons?
- (A) Simmons was very old.
- (B) Simmons could make egrets.
- (C) Simmons taught young people.
- (D) Simmons was an artist.

9. How old was Philip Simmons when he became a blacksmith apprentice?
- (A) 25
- (B) 13
- (C) 18
- (D) 10

10. Who is John Vlach?
- (A) an apprentice
- (B) a blacksmith who needs ideas
- (C) someone who studies traditional crafts
- (D) an inspector from the government

11. The greatest test of Philip Simmons' career was to _____ .
- (A) make the Snake Gate in Charleston
- (B) make a gate in Washington, D.C.
- (C) forge an egret
- (D) demonstrate his forging skills to visitors

12. Why did Simmons agree to Vlach's offer?
- (A) Simmons thought he could make something that he could sell later.
- (B) Simmons could take his own tools to Washington with him.
- (C) Simmons thought he might become well known outside of Charleston.
- (D) Simmons wanted to get more business from the fair.

© Harcourt

13. When did Simmons finally decide what kind of gate he should make at the Festival of American Folklife?
- (A) six weeks before the festival
- (B) at the festival
- (C) on the plane to the festival
- (D) He decided not to make anything at the festival.

14. How did Simmons solve the problem of the star's center point?
- (A) by ignoring the 20 degrees it was off center
- (B) by cutting the star out and welding it in again
- (C) by telling everyone that it was pointing straight up
- (D) by saying that a star shines many different ways

15. Why was Simmons given a Heritage Fellowship?
- (A) John Vlach liked him.
- (B) He was invited to Washington, D.C.
- (C) His artistic skill was a national treasure.
- (D) He had already won many awards.

16. "Simmons has taught at least five apprentices." In this selection, an *apprentice* is _____ .
- (A) someone learning to be a blacksmith
- (B) a blacksmith demonstrating for visitors
- (C) a visitor watching a blacksmith
- (D) a cousin of Philip Simmons

17. What did the Smithsonian do with the Star and Fish Gate?
- (A) The museum left the gate in Philip Simmons' shop.
- (B) The gate traveled to museums around the United States.
- (C) The gate was exhibited in the Smithsonian Institution in Washington, D.C.
- (D) The gate was shown to tourists in Charleston.

Practice Book
Timeless Treasures

18. Why was Charleston the last place to honor Philip Simmons?

(A) The Smithsonian would not let any other organization honor Mr. Simmons.

(B) Philip Simmons trained more blacksmiths in Charleston.

(C) He received the South Carolina Folk Heritage Award.

(D) His talent was taken for granted in his hometown.

19. How did the Historic Charleston Foundation make Philip Simmons' greatest wish come true?

_____

_____

_____

_____

_____

_____

_____

20. Philip Simmons said, "You got to teach kids while the sap is young, just like you got to beat the iron while it's hot." What did he mean?

_____

_____

_____

_____

_____

_____

_____

_____

Seventh Grade

Directions: For items 1–18, fill in the circle in front of the correct answer.
For items 19–20, write the answer.

Vocabulary

1. Did you sign up for speech or art as your _____ course?
Ⓐ acquaintance   Ⓑ passive
Ⓒ elective   Ⓓ restrained

2. We can tell from the _____ on your face that you are unhappy about something.
Ⓐ priority   Ⓑ scowl
Ⓒ screen   Ⓓ reflection

3. The minor setback did not weaken her _____ that she was doing the right thing.
Ⓐ conviction   Ⓑ depression
Ⓒ generation   Ⓓ conjunction

4. The busy students _____ about, putting up decorations for the party.
Ⓐ contained   Ⓑ bustled
Ⓒ bribed   Ⓓ mentioned

5. With _____ , Mike volunteered a guess at the answer to the teacher's question.
Ⓐ sponges   Ⓑ shame
Ⓒ intervals   Ⓓ uncertainty

6. The little boy _____ admitted he had thrown the ball through the window accidentally.
Ⓐ sheepishly   Ⓑ boldly
Ⓒ drastically   Ⓓ gradually

7. The jet engine _____ the plane into the sky and on to Europe.
Ⓐ flexed   Ⓑ bailed
Ⓒ wailed   Ⓓ propelled

Comprehension

8. This selection takes place _____.
- Ⓐ on the first day of school in the seventh grade
- Ⓑ on the last day of school in the sixth grade
- Ⓒ on the first day of school in the sixth grade
- Ⓓ in catechism class at Saint Theresa's Church

9. Victor would probably say that France is _____ .
- Ⓐ nicer than Fresno
- Ⓑ too cold
- Ⓒ an unfriendly country
- Ⓓ too heavily populated

10. Why is Victor taking French?
- Ⓐ His friend Michael Torres is taking it.
- Ⓑ The girl he likes is taking it.
- Ⓒ He wants a job using languages when he grows up.
- Ⓓ He likes the way it sounds.

11. How do Victor and Michael earn money for their school clothes?
- Ⓐ by washing cars
- Ⓑ by mowing lawns
- Ⓒ by working at the public library
- Ⓓ by picking grapes

12. Which of the following happens during homeroom period?
- Ⓐ Victor tries to scowl.
- Ⓑ Victor finds out that Teresa is in his English class.
- Ⓒ Victor asks Teresa how her summer was.
- Ⓓ Victor sees Teresa.

13. How does Victor embarrass himself in English class?

   Ⓐ He just stays quiet when asked a question.

   Ⓑ He gives a wrong answer.

   Ⓒ He answers a question with Teresa's name.

   Ⓓ He practices scowling instead of paying attention.

14. What is Victor's first class after lunch?

   Ⓐ biology

   Ⓑ French

   Ⓒ math

   Ⓓ social studies

15. Why do Victor and Teresa have to sit in the front in French class?

   Ⓐ The back seats are already taken.

   Ⓑ They are late, so Mr. Bueller makes them sit in front.

   Ⓒ Their friends save two seats together for them.

   Ⓓ All students have assigned seats.

16. What can the reader tell for certain about Michael's scowling?

   Ⓐ It makes girls ignore him.

   Ⓑ Girls find his scowling attractive.

   Ⓒ Girls think his scowling is strange.

   Ⓓ It attracts attention.

17. Think about how Mr. Bueller treats Victor in front of Teresa. Which word best describes this teacher?

   Ⓐ cruel

   Ⓑ considerate

   Ⓒ insensitive

   Ⓓ indifferent

18. How does Teresa seem to feel about Victor?

   Ⓐ She thinks he is ridiculous.

   Ⓑ She wishes he would leave her alone.

   Ⓒ She is embarrassed that he likes her.

   Ⓓ She likes talking to him.

19. Where did Victor first start liking Teresa?

_____

_____

_____

_____

_____

_____

_____

_____

_____

_____

20. What special interest does Teresa ask the homeroom teacher about?

_____

_____

_____

_____

_____

_____

_____

_____

_____

_____

© Harcourt

My Name Is San Ho

Directions: For items 1–18, fill in the circle in front of the correct answer.
For items 19–20, write the answer.

Vocabulary

1. My friend _____ to me to join the others on the baseball field.
(A) rugged
(B) impressed
(C) gestured
(D) detected

2. Everyone is _____ by the disappearance of all the jewelry from the safe.
(A) mystified
(B) bustled
(C) favored
(D) trotted

3. We set a _____ date for the party until we could clear the time with the guest of honor.
(A) convicted
(B) tentative
(C) discouraging
(D) melodious

4. After our terrible defeat, the team was trying to _____ the courage to smile and be cheerful.
(A) propose
(B) blush
(C) perchance
(D) muster

5. The _____ of the woman's speech was not apparent until years later when she made an important discovery in medicine.
(A) generation
(B) discouragement
(C) dependence
(D) significance

6. The teacher _____ accepted the praise and the present from her students.
(A) angrily
(B) appreciatively
(C) gradually
(D) hysterically

Comprehension

7. This selection takes place mostly in _____ .
   (A) Saigon
   (B) Philadelphia
   (C) Viet Nam
   (D) New York

8. Who does San Ho live with?
   (A) his mother and father
   (B) his mother and stepfather
   (C) his grandparents
   (D) adoptive parents

9. Which word best describes how San Ho feels at the beginning of the selection?
   (A) happy
   (B) frustrated
   (C) angry
   (D) tired

10. What responsibility is placed on San Ho during gym class?
   (A) passing the batons to the teams
   (B) being the only runner on one team
   (C) winning the race for his team
   (D) cheering for his team

11. San Ho doesn't dare look to see where his opponent is because he _____ .
   (A) can see a runner in front of him
   (B) doesn't want to lose time turning around
   (C) hears his team shouting at him to run faster
   (D) sees the runner beside him

12. Besides pride in winning the race, San Ho feels good because now he feels like _____ .

   Ⓐ he is still a stranger in school

   Ⓑ he can speak English

   Ⓒ Bruce is angry with him

   Ⓓ he is part of his class

13. In this selection a hamlet is a _____ .

   Ⓐ small city

   Ⓑ large city

   Ⓒ large town

   Ⓓ small village

14. What present does San Ho receive from Stephen?

   Ⓐ a red bike

   Ⓑ a green bike

   Ⓒ a basketball

   Ⓓ a red scooter

15. San Ho practices talking in English all the following ways **except** by _____ .

   Ⓐ talking into a tape recorder

   Ⓑ talking with Stephen

   Ⓒ acting in a school play

   Ⓓ reading with his mother

16. How is doing math in America different for San Ho than doing math in Vietnam?

   Ⓐ In America he uses an abacus to add.

   Ⓑ In Vietnam he uses a stick and pebbles for computing.

   Ⓒ In America he can't use an abacus.

   Ⓓ In Vietnam he is good in math and does well on quizzes.

17. Which word best describes how San Ho feels about the ending of the school year?

Ⓐ sorry

Ⓑ delighted

Ⓒ important

Ⓓ ashamed

18. This selection is most like _____ story.

Ⓐ a biographical

Ⓑ an autobiographical

Ⓒ an essay

Ⓓ a realistic fiction

19. How is San Ho's bicycle different from those he has seen in Vietnam?

_____

_____

_____

_____

_____

_____

_____

20. Why doesn't San Ho want the school year to end?

_____

_____

_____

_____

_____

_____

_____

_____

Out of Darkness: The Story of Louis Braille

Directions: For items 1–18, fill in the circle in front of the correct answer. For items 19–20, write the answer.

Vocabulary

1. It is a good idea to begin a running program _____, going a little farther each day until you can run your desired distance.
   - Ⓐ greedily
   - Ⓑ ignorantly
   - Ⓒ gradually
   - Ⓓ casually

2. Jerry _____ a code that he and his friends could use to send secret messages.
   - Ⓐ devised
   - Ⓑ closed
   - Ⓒ sympathized
   - Ⓓ occupied

3. The surgeon operated with _____, knowing that the slightest slip could cause injury.
   - Ⓐ petition
   - Ⓑ attraction
   - Ⓒ opinion
   - Ⓓ precision

4. My sister, who is away at college, lives in a _____ there.
   - Ⓐ cavity
   - Ⓑ dormitory
   - Ⓒ passageway
   - Ⓓ district

5. Each blind student has a _____, which is used for writing.
   - Ⓐ specialty
   - Ⓑ wedge
   - Ⓒ stylus
   - Ⓓ mosaic

6. The secretary of the club _____ her notes from the meeting into a large notebook.
   - Ⓐ transcribed
   - Ⓑ reconstructed
   - Ⓒ propelled
   - Ⓓ disguised

Comprehension

7. Why did Louis frequently fall asleep in class?

Ⓐ The classes were not challenging enough.

Ⓑ He was sickly and got tired easily.

Ⓒ He stayed up all night working on his reading system.

Ⓓ The school allowed students to sleep only six hours each night.

8. Why was Louis's mother worried about him when he came home on vacation?

Ⓐ He didn't look well and had a cough.

Ⓑ He seldom slept.

Ⓒ He had lost interest in his schoolwork.

Ⓓ He spent too much time alone.

9. Louis found all the following disadvantages with sonography **except** that it _____ .

Ⓐ used both dots and dashes

Ⓑ took too many symbols to represent a word

Ⓒ was very fast and easy to use

Ⓓ had no symbols for numbers and punctuation

10. How long did Louis work on his reading system before he presented it to Dr. Pignier?

Ⓐ fifteen years

Ⓑ an entire summer vacation

Ⓒ an entire school year

Ⓓ three years

11. Which word best describes Dr. Pignier's reaction to Louis's system?

Ⓐ subdued   Ⓑ enthusiastic

Ⓒ encouraging   Ⓓ negative

© Harcourt

12. How was Braille's code for blind readers different than sonography?
  (A) It was based on sounds and letters.
  (B) Each letter had a different number of dashes.
  (C) Each letter took up the space of one fingertip.
  (D) He added dashes for numbers and spelling.

13. Why did Braille decide not to use dashes in his system?
  (A) Dashes were hard to engrave.
  (B) Dashes were difficult to feel.
  (C) Dashes took up too much space.
  (D) Dashes were easily confused with dots.

14. "Within this cell, Louis worked out different arrangements of dots." In this selection, *cell* means _____ .
  (A) a single room in a prison
  (B) the smallest part of an organization
  (C) a cup or jar used to make electricity
  (D) a small amount of space with boundaries

15. According to the selection, what do the first ten characters of Louis's system represent?
  (A) just the first ten letters of the alphabet
  (B) the first ten letters of the alphabet and ten Arabic numerals
  (C) just ten Arabic numerals
  (D) ten Arabic numerals and punctuation

16. All the following are represented by single characters in Louis's system except _____ .
  (A) musical notations
  (B) contractions
  (C) some common words
  (D) names of colors

Practice Book
Timeless Treasures

17. Which tool is used to punch Braille dots in paper?

Ⓐ a sliding rule

Ⓑ a frame

Ⓒ a stylus

Ⓓ a pen point

18. Braille is written from right to left, but it is read from _____ .

Ⓐ left to right

Ⓑ right to left

Ⓒ top to bottom

Ⓓ bottom to top

19. What did Louis Braille do after he graduated from school?

_____

_____

_____

_____

_____

_____

_____

20. What is the *darkness* that this selection's title refers to?

_____

_____

_____

_____

_____

_____

_____

_____

Anne of Green Gables

Directions: For items 1–18, fill in the circle in front of the correct answer. For items 19–20, write the answer.

Vocabulary

1. I was overcome by an _____ urge to go to the beach.
- (A) irresistible
- (B) embezzled
- (C) implored
- (D) undeveloped

2. The actor bowed _____ to the cheering crowd before he exited the stage.
- (A) shrilly
- (B) dramatically
- (C) selfishly
- (D) vocally

3. The witness _____ swore to tell the truth, the whole truth, and nothing but the truth.
- (A) mildly
- (B) solemnly
- (C) mutually
- (D) flexibly

4. The nervous director was all a _____ when he tried to get the cast in place for the opening number.
- (A) fluster
- (B) snooping
- (C) novelty
- (D) patriot

5. The girl had a _____ expression on her face when her name was called to come forward and receive first prize.
- (A) devised
- (B) enterprising
- (C) bewildered
- (D) comparative

6. Tasting the delicious homemade ice cream was truly _____ to Anne.
- (A) sublime
- (B) sheepish
- (C) awful
- (D) rancid

Practice Book
Timeless Treasures

Comprehension

7. Where does the play take place?
- Ⓐ on a farm
- Ⓑ in an orphanage
- Ⓒ at a picnic
- Ⓓ in a small town

8. Why is there a disagreement between Matthew and Marilla when he brings Anne home for the first time?
- Ⓐ Marilla is hoping for an older child, but Matthew brings a baby instead.
- Ⓑ Marilla is expecting hired help, but Matthew brings an orphan instead.
- Ⓒ Matthew has arranged to adopt a boy, not a girl.
- Ⓓ Matthew wants to adopt Anne, but Marilla is hesitant.

9. Anne feels she is unable to eat supper the first night at the Curberts' house because she _____ .
- Ⓐ isn't hungry
- Ⓑ is upset that they wanted a boy instead of her
- Ⓒ has a lump in her throat
- Ⓓ is stubborn

10. Which word best describes Anne?
- Ⓐ quiet
- Ⓑ calm
- Ⓓ dramatic
- Ⓓ shy

11. Which describes how Anne looks?
- Ⓐ red-haired, clumsy, plump
- Ⓑ red-haired, freckled, skinny
- Ⓒ raven-haired, freckled, skinny
- Ⓓ raven-haired, rosy-cheeked, plump

12. What does the meeting with Mrs. Lynde reveal about Anne?
- (A) She is very polite.
- (B) She is noisy.
- (C) She has a temper.
- (D) She is a quiet person.

13. When Anne and Diana sit at the front of the stage, where are they supposed to be?
- (A) in Avonlea
- (B) in the sitting room
- (C) in the flower garden
- (D) in the barn

14. For Anne, what is the most exciting thing about the Sunday School picnic?
- (A) going for a boat ride
- (B) eating a picnic lunch
- (C) riding to the picnic
- (D) having ice cream

15. Why does Anne confess to something she hasn't done?
- (A) She is sure that she's telling the truth.
- (B) She thinks that Marilla will let her go to the picnic if she confesses.
- (C) She doesn't want Diana to be blamed.
- (D) She is upset that she can't remember exactly what happened.

16. What two things go wrong for Anne in the last scene?
- (A) She dyes her hair green and puts cough syrup in the cake.
- (B) She loses Marilla's brooch and doesn't go to the picnic.
- (C) She lies to Marilla and makes Diana angry.
- (D) She is disrespectful to Mrs. Lynde; and she's a girl, not a boy.

Practice Book
Timeless Treasures

17. Once they know Anne, people generally think that she is _____.

Ⓐ dull

Ⓑ annoying

Ⓒ charming

Ⓓ ridiculous

18. About how much time passes during the play?

Ⓐ one day

Ⓑ one week

Ⓒ one month

Ⓓ one year

19. Why does Anne think that the spelling of her name is so important?

_____

_____

_____

_____

_____

_____

_____

_____

20. How would you describe how Anne talks?

_____

_____

_____

_____

_____

_____

_____

_____

Cowboys: Roundup on an American Ranch

Directions: For items 1–18, fill in the circle in front of the correct answer. For items 19–20, write the answer.

Vocabulary

1. Our livestock were _____ for the night so that they could not wander away.
   - (A) hired
   - (B) informed
   - (C) corralled
   - (D) vowed

2. Once John passed the entrance requirement, he became a _____ member of the club.
   - (A) fullfledged
   - (B) rejected
   - (C) previous
   - (D) resigned

3. My horse Trixie can be _____ when she feels like it, and you can't get her to do a thing you want.
   - (A) contagious
   - (B) ornery
   - (C) massive
   - (D) modern

4. The waitress in the restaurant was _____ with our request and served dessert before the meal.
   - (A) edible
   - (B) remote
   - (C) previous
   - (D) compliant

5. The actor created a _____ so the stage crew could change the scenery.
   - (A) division
   - (B) diversion
   - (C) conviction
   - (D) transmission

6. The rugged terrain has many _____ plants we have to circumvent to avoid hurting the horses.
   - (A) glaring
   - (B) craggy
   - (C) cactus
   - (D) bald

7. The heavy rain _____ the soil and reaches the deep roots of the dried-out crops.

   Ⓐ permeates

   Ⓑ stains

   Ⓒ excavates

   Ⓓ isolates

Comprehension

8. What proves Leedro's suspicion that his horse has hurt her ankle?

   Ⓐ He feels a bump on her ankle.

   Ⓑ She won't leave her pen.

   Ⓒ Her ankle feels hot when he touches it.

   Ⓓ She won't let him put her bridle on.

9. Why does Leedro's father want to sell off a lot of cattle?

   Ⓐ so they won't die of thirst

   Ⓑ because they're fat

   Ⓒ because he needs money to keep his ranch

   Ⓓ because he is already late rounding them up

10. Who owns the ranch in this selection?

   Ⓐ Colter Eby

   Ⓑ Larry Eby

   Ⓒ Randy Biebelle

   Ⓓ Tom Brown

11. Why does the dead calf confirm that there is a drought?

   Ⓐ The calf died from thirst.

   Ⓑ The calf's mother did not have enough milk for it.

   Ⓒ It was killed by a predator suffering from hunger because of the drought.

   Ⓓ A rattlesnake killed it.

© Harcourt

12. "I spread the cattle out, only about eight or ten on each section." In this selection, *section* means a _____ .

(A) separate part of something written, such as a newspaper

(B) very thin slice of something to look at under a microscope

(C) part of an orchestra that has all the same kind of instrument

(D) part of a larger piece of land

13. Leedro's father puts only eight to ten cows on each section so the cattle _____ .

(A) are easier to round up

(B) are less likely to stampede

(C) don't crowd the watering holes

(D) do not overgraze the land

14. How do the cowboys spend their time while at The Box?

(A) refreshing themselves and their horses

(B) counting cattle

(C) feeding the cattle and horses

(D) waiting for cowboys who are retrieving runaways

15. Why does the ranch have windmills?

(A) to pump water from underground springs

(B) to show how fast the wind is blowing

(C) to show if a storm is coming

(D) to pump water from creeks into watering troughs

16. For the author, what do the groups of cattle heading toward Tom Brown Basin look like?

(A) patches of a quilt

(B) marbles on a table

(C) branches of a tree

(D) spokes of a wheel

Practice Book
Timeless Treasures

17. To keep the cattle strung out in an uneven line, some cowboys ride _____ .

Ⓐ point

Ⓑ swing

Ⓒ flank

Ⓓ and constantly hit the cattle with ropes

18. In writing this selection, the author wants to tell about what happens _____ .

Ⓐ on a cattle roundup

Ⓑ in training a young colt

Ⓒ when a ranch is divided into sections

Ⓓ when a rancher thinks as a cow

19. Why do some cowboys ride flank?

_____

_____

_____

_____

_____

_____

20. In the author's opinion, why is driving the herd from Tom Brown Basin to the next water hole the most fun?

_____

_____

_____

_____

_____

_____

© Harcourt

Atlas in the Round

Directions: For items 1–18, fill in the circle in front of the correct answer. For items 19–20, write the answer.

Vocabulary

1. When we made a time capsule, we put everything in a waterproof _____ .
- Ⓐ cylinder
- Ⓑ photograph
- Ⓒ newspaper
- Ⓓ building

2. At the new restaurant, the portions were almost _____ in size.
- Ⓐ delicious
- Ⓑ steaming
- Ⓒ spicy
- Ⓓ microscopic

3. The window was so dirty and scratched, it was no longer _____ .
- Ⓐ open
- Ⓑ secure
- Ⓒ transparent
- Ⓓ glass

4. It is _____ in our family to have a family reunion every summer in July.
- Ⓐ precision
- Ⓑ transparent
- Ⓒ traditional
- Ⓓ technical

5. It was frightening to see the two cars _____ on the icy highway.
- Ⓐ invite
- Ⓑ collide
- Ⓒ stop
- Ⓓ stretch

6. A particular kind of lily will bloom even when _____ in water.
- Ⓐ overhead
- Ⓑ absent
- Ⓒ under
- Ⓓ submerged

Practice Book
Timeless Treasures

Comprehension

7. The main idea of this selection is _____ .
(A) how the physical features of Earth have changed
(B) how the four oceans of Earth were formed
(C) Earth as a ball of rock
(D) that there are two kinds of maps

8. The major problem with showing Earth on a flat map is _____ .
(A) Earth is not flat and can't be shown accurately on a flat map
(B) flat maps work better in trying to find how to get between two places
(C) it is possible to show a round surface on a flat piece of paper
(D) a flat map divides Earth into segments

9. All of the following can be found on the floor of the oceans **except** _____ .
(A) mountains   (B) plains
(C) valleys   (D) still water

10. The largest ocean on Earth is the _____ Ocean.
(A) Atlantic
(B) Indian
(C) Arctic
(D) Pacific

11. Earth was formed about _____ years ago.
(A) 1.5 million
(B) 4.6 billion
(C) 220 million
(D) 65 billion

12. According to this selection, which of the following is a true statement?
(A) Dinosaurs lived before amphibians.
(B) Amphibians were the first land animals.
(C) Mammals lived before amphibians.
(D) No fossils of microscopic organisms have been found.

© Harcourt

Practice Book
Timeless Treasures

13. An earthquake is caused by _____ .
Ⓐ the edges of the plates breaking
Ⓑ plates moving sideways
Ⓒ plates moving suddenly
Ⓓ currents moving the plates

14. The Hawaiian Islands are mountainous because they are made of _____ .
Ⓐ atolls
Ⓑ volcanoes
Ⓒ coral
Ⓓ ocean ridges

15. In this selection, *extinct* means _____ .
Ⓐ shallow
Ⓑ active
Ⓒ dead
Ⓓ low-lying

16. According to this selection, the chief feature of the Atlantic Ocean is _____ .
Ⓐ a mountain range running north-south in the ocean
Ⓑ the Caribbean Sea
Ⓒ Newfoundland and Iceland
Ⓓ it has been overfished

17. About 180 million years ago, India and the _____ were neighbors.
Ⓐ North Pole
Ⓑ Equator
Ⓒ South Pole
Ⓓ Pacific Ocean

18. Today the Arctic area is made up of all of the following **except** _____ .
Ⓐ Europe
Ⓑ Australia
Ⓒ North America
Ⓓ Northern Asia

Practice Book
Timeless Treasures

19. How much of the Earth's surface is made up of water? How much is made up of land?

_____

_____

_____

_____

_____

_____

_____

_____

_____

20. Why is the Atlantic Ocean growing about an inch a year?

_____

_____

_____

_____

_____

_____

_____

_____

_____

_____

Dive! My Adventure in the Deep Frontier

Directions: For items 1–18, fill in the circle in front of the correct answer. For items 19–20, write the answer.

Vocabulary

1. The pressure _____ on my air tank was broken, so my dive was canceled.
   - Ⓐ cooker
   - Ⓑ gauge
   - Ⓒ remote
   - Ⓓ vacuum

2. If the fog would only _____, our flight would not be delayed.
   - Ⓐ dissipate
   - Ⓑ increase
   - Ⓒ temperature
   - Ⓓ tighten

3. I signed up to be a crew member on a _____ boat to explore shipwrecks.
   - Ⓐ final
   - Ⓑ grocery
   - Ⓒ leisure
   - Ⓓ salvage

4. When I went to the islands, sunshine and beautiful beaches _____ .
   - Ⓐ pleasure
   - Ⓑ disappeared
   - Ⓒ abounded
   - Ⓓ serviced

5. The rich _____ in our community was celebrated on Multicultural Day.
   - Ⓐ diversity
   - Ⓑ salaries
   - Ⓒ moment
   - Ⓓ neighborhoods

6. My brother claims that an _____ guitar sounds better than any other.
   - Ⓐ orange
   - Ⓑ orderly
   - Ⓒ athletic
   - Ⓓ acoustic

7. We tested the _____ of soap and wood by putting them in water.
   - Ⓐ observation
   - Ⓑ buoyancy
   - Ⓒ telephone
   - Ⓓ temperature

Comprehension

8. In this selection a *submersible* is _____ .
   - Ⓐ a robot that goes underwater
   - Ⓑ an underwater science lab
   - Ⓒ diving gear
   - Ⓓ similar to a small submarine

9. To *decompress* in deep water means to _____ .
   - Ⓐ obtain additional oxygen under water
   - Ⓑ dissipate the nitrogen buildup in a diver's blood
   - Ⓒ read a depth gauge
   - Ⓓ enter a submersible

10. Jim is similar to _____ .
    - Ⓐ an underwater lab
    - Ⓑ a type of submarine
    - Ⓒ an astronaut's spacesuit
    - Ⓓ a 1,000-pound helmet

11. The author of this selection speculates that there may be living creatures on one of Jupiter's moons because _____ .
    - Ⓐ there is water on that moon
    - Ⓑ scientists met people who had visited there
    - Ⓒ astronauts found animal fossils there
    - Ⓓ Europa is a moon of Jupiter

12. What is the average depth of the ocean?
    - Ⓐ 1,250 feet
    - Ⓑ 2.5 miles
    - Ⓒ 1,300,000 feet
    - Ⓓ 5 miles

© Harcourt

Practice Book
Timeless Treasures

13. The deepest part of the ocean, which is east of the Philippines, has been visited _____ .

Ⓐ by dozens of researchers

Ⓑ nearly every year since 1960

Ⓒ by crews drilling for oil

Ⓓ by only two people

14. Dolphins and whales "see" because of their _____ .

Ⓐ sonar

Ⓑ keen vision

Ⓒ sense of touch

Ⓓ mechanical arms

15. What was the first step in building *Deep Rover?*

Ⓐ testing it in the ocean

Ⓑ starting a company

Ⓒ naming the submersible

Ⓓ a basic design

16. According to this selection, gelatinous creatures are _____ .

Ⓐ shrimp

Ⓑ fish

Ⓒ jellyfish

Ⓓ octopuses

17. What "surprise" creature does the author find at the bottom of the sea?

Ⓐ sponges

Ⓑ silver-red fish

Ⓒ a soda can

Ⓓ an octopus

18. *Deep Rover* is made from a clear material _____ .

Ⓐ so that the diver can see into the ocean

Ⓑ so that the pressure will be equalized

Ⓒ because it's easier to add a headlight to plastic

Ⓓ because the author wanted it that way

Practice Book
Timeless Treasures

19. How does the author feel about finding a soda can in the bottom of the ocean?

_____

_____

_____

_____

_____

_____

_____

_____

_____

_____

20. Why do you think the author used "Frontier" as part of the title of the selection?

_____

_____

_____

_____

_____

_____

_____

_____

_____

_____

I Want to Be an Astronaut

Directions: For items 1–18, fill in the circle in front of the correct answer. For items 19–20, write the answer.

Vocabulary

1. Jeff has a new car with a computerized _____ system to show locations.
- (A) seating
- (B) underwater
- (C) education
- (D) navigation

2. Gymnasiums are sports _____ .
- (A) tracks
- (B) notebooks
- (C) facilities
- (D) writers

3. The special agent was given a top-secret _____ in Europe.
- (A) mission
- (B) jungle
- (C) vocabulary
- (D) advertisement

4. The ambulance had to _____ through heavy traffic to get to the hospital.
- (A) stall
- (B) leak
- (C) spark
- (D) maneuver

5. Ramon has a video game that is a _____ of a football game.
- (A) quiz
- (B) simulation
- (C) conflict
- (D) halftime

Practice Book
Timeless Treasures

6. My dad's office has the latest in _____ computer equipment.
   (A) high-tech
   (B) antique
   (C) exercise
   (D) surgical

Comprehension

7. "Astronauts Harris and Foale are on their way out of the shuttle orbiter for some extravehicular activity." In this selection, *extra* in *extravehicular* means _____ .
   (A) outside
   (B) inside
   (C) beside
   (D) on the opposite side of

8. How are the jobs of a payload crew member and a mission specialist alike?
   (A) They help keep the space vehicle in good working shape.
   (B) They are on the ship only to observe.
   (C) They are government officials who check efficiency.
   (D) They perform experiments during the flight.

9. Astronauts are typically trained in all the following fields **except** _____ .
   (A) science
   (B) mathematics
   (C) art
   (D) engineering

10. Which is true about astronauts living in space?
   (A) They cannot keep clean.
   (B) They wear space suits all the time.
   (C) They have to strap almost everything down.
   (D) They spend all their time working or sleeping.

© Harcourt

11. In this selection, the word *queasy* describes feeling _____ .
Ⓐ healthy
Ⓑ cheerful
Ⓒ nauseous
Ⓓ sleepy

12. Where are astronaut training facilities in the United States?
Ⓐ in the Northeast
Ⓑ along the Pacific coast
Ⓒ in the Midwest
Ⓓ in the South

13. Why do astronauts sometimes train in giant pools?
Ⓐ Working against water resistance builds strength.
Ⓑ Working in water feels similar to working in space.
Ⓒ They are practicing for an unexpected water leak in space.
Ⓓ They get used to their space suits under water.

14. Why do astronauts take trips in planes that suddenly dive 11,000 feet?
Ⓐ to experience weightlessness
Ⓑ to practice regaining control of the plane
Ⓒ to use their problem-solving skills
Ⓓ to practice their teamwork

15. What do astronauts have to learn in case of a crash landing?
Ⓐ several languages
Ⓑ land and sea survival skills
Ⓒ enduring weightlessness
Ⓓ breathing without oxygen

16. Students at a space camp do all the following **except** _____ .
Ⓐ fly on a real space mission
Ⓑ find out about the space program
Ⓒ do teamwork and problem-solving exercises
Ⓓ learn about the science of spaceflight

17. The deaths of seven astronauts in 1986 resulted in the founding of _____ .

  (A) NASA's Can Do program

  (B) the Young Astronauts program

  (C) NASA's Teacher Resource Centers

  (D) the Challenger Center

18. To become an astronaut requires all the following **except** _____ .

  (A) years of training

  (B) advanced education

  (C) championship athletic ability

  (D) hard work

19. Why is good teamwork an important skill for astronauts?

_____

_____

_____

_____

_____

_____

_____

20. Why do astronauts need good problem-solving skills?

_____

_____

_____

_____

_____

_____

_____

Practice Book
Timeless Treasures

Directions: For items 1–18, fill in the circle in front of the correct answer. For items 19–20, write the answer.

Vocabulary

1. During the snowstorm, my friends and I _____ each other with snowballs.
- Ⓐ soaked
- Ⓑ bombarded
- Ⓒ bored
- Ⓓ understood

2. When our _____ broke, we could no longer get on the Internet.
- Ⓐ printer
- Ⓑ television
- Ⓒ modem
- Ⓓ dishwasher

3. An _____ Web site is one in which you make your own selections for where to go and what to read.
- Ⓐ interactive
- Ⓑ according
- Ⓒ accidental
- Ⓓ inside

4. A television show is an example of a _____ from a TV station.
- Ⓐ package
- Ⓑ surrender
- Ⓒ boost
- Ⓓ transmission

5. My parents allow me to go _____ only when my homework is finished.
- Ⓐ online
- Ⓑ photograph
- Ⓒ compliant
- Ⓓ unconscious

6. Rudy had a _____ of phone calls about the scooter he wanted to sell.
- Ⓐ scene
- Ⓑ symptom
- Ⓒ document
- Ⓓ barrage

Comprehension

7. Say "Goodbye snail-mail, hello e-mail." In this selection, *e-mail* means _____ .

   Ⓐ easy mail

   Ⓑ early mail

   Ⓒ everyday mail

   Ⓓ electronic mail

8. According to the selection, how long does it usually take an e-mail message to reach its destination?

   Ⓐ a few minutes

   Ⓑ a few seconds

   Ⓒ several hours

   Ⓓ one or two days

9. Cybersurfers refer to traditional mail as *snail-mail* because _____ .

   Ⓐ it might take days to reach the person

   Ⓑ it arrives special delivery

   Ⓒ snails are speedy animals

   Ⓓ it is faster than the pony express

10. In an e-mail address, the user's ID is separated from the user's location by _____ .

   Ⓐ an exclamation point

   Ⓑ a colon

   Ⓒ an "at" symbol

   Ⓓ a period, or "dot"

11. Which of the following is true about e-mail?

   Ⓐ The Internet breaks e-mail messages into smaller, addressed packets of information.

   Ⓑ E-mail messages going long distances need longer addresses than local e-mail.

   Ⓒ E-mail messages are frequently lost for short periods of time.

   Ⓓ It is not possible to send attachments with e-mail.

Practice Book
Timeless Treasures

12. In this selection, "spamming" refers to _____ .

   Ⓐ eating a sandwich made with canned meat

   Ⓑ using someone's e-mail address to pull a prank

   Ⓒ your telephone area code

   Ⓓ a bowl of alphabet soup

13. Which action on the Net would probably cause a person to get flamed?

   Ⓐ answering e-mail quickly

   Ⓑ using underlined type

   Ⓒ using boldface type

   Ⓓ calling someone an ugly name

14. How can a user tell what is hypertext?

   Ⓐ The words are in larger type.

   Ⓑ The words are underlined or in a different color.

   Ⓒ An arrow appears before the hypertext.

   Ⓓ The words are marked by *(HTTP)*.

15. What happens when someone surfing the Net clicks on hypertext?

   Ⓐ The text immediately becomes larger and easier to read.

   Ⓑ The user goes to related information on the Web.

   Ⓒ The computer goes back to the previous screen.

   Ⓓ The computer immediately defines the word.

16. Which of the following best helps surfers quickly return to sites they like?

   Ⓐ search engines

   Ⓑ home pages

   Ⓒ bookmarks

   Ⓓ a mouse

17. When using the Net, which is probably safe to tell a stranger?

   Ⓐ what your home address is

   Ⓑ where your parents work

   Ⓒ what your best friend's phone number is

   Ⓓ what you like to do

Practice Book
Timeless Treasures

18. How can you protect your computer from getting "sick"?

   Ⓐ by using a virus checker

   Ⓑ by turning your computer off every day

   Ⓒ by sending disgusting messages back to the people who sent them

   Ⓓ by using a browser

19. What does "surfing the Net" mean?

_____

_____

_____

_____

_____

_____

_____

_____

20. What computer language do many programmers use to design Web home pages?

_____

_____

_____

_____

_____

_____

_____

_____

© Harcourt

Name _____ Date _____

The Case of the Shining Blue Planet

Directions: For items 1–18, fill in the circle in front of the correct answer. For items 19–20, write the answer.

Vocabulary

1. The discovery that the world is round is considered a _____ in geography.
   Ⓐ argument   Ⓑ breakthrough
   Ⓒ astronaut   Ⓓ title

2. Brian totally _____ his brother's advice not to play ball inside the house.
   Ⓐ disregarded
   Ⓑ canceled
   Ⓒ translated
   Ⓓ reserved

3. A panel discussion between a Russian _____ and an American astronaut was held in our school.
   Ⓐ driver
   Ⓑ conductor
   Ⓒ cosmonaut
   Ⓓ passenger

4. A _____ was launched into space so we could make better weather predictions.
   Ⓐ spacesuit
   Ⓑ docking
   Ⓒ jetpack
   Ⓓ satellite

5. There are many _____ for curing the common cold, but it usually takes seven days.
   Ⓐ rhymes
   Ⓑ decorations
   Ⓒ elements
   Ⓓ formulas

Practice Book
Timeless Treasures

6. After their final out in the baseball game, the losing team walked _____ off the field.

(A) happily   (B) awake

(C) dejectedly   (D) likely

7. Chris often _____ in a tutoring session after school for extra help in math.

(A) sleeps

(B) enrolls

(C) rents

(D) irons

8. When the _____ broke in flight, the pilot was very concerned.

(A) altimeter

(B) expert

(C) mathematician

(D) eggs

Comprehension

9. What does Stanley want Einstein to see?

(A) a photo of a dinosaur

(B) his robot

(C) information on a space alien

(D) his discovery on the Internet

10. How does Einstein feel about offers on the Internet?

(A) angry

(B) excited

(C) amused

(D) suspicious

11. Which best describes Einstein's kidding?

(A) mean

(B) educational

(C) friendly

(D) foolish

12. Why is Stanley interested in Dr. K.'s website?

  Ⓐ Stanley hopes to perform experiments in space.

  Ⓑ Stanley wants Dr. K.'s photos of the earth.

  Ⓒ Stanley plans to be an astronaut some day.

  Ⓓ Stanley wants to learn about spy research.

13. How do Stanley and Einstein feel about Dr. K.'s fee for sending up a satellite?

  Ⓐ There should be no fee.

  Ⓑ It's the right amount of money.

  Ⓒ It's not enough money.

  Ⓓ It's too much money.

14. Dr. K. sent Stanley some mathematical formulas. How much does Stanley learn from them about the satellite project?

  Ⓐ nothing

  Ⓑ a little

  Ⓒ a lot

  Ⓓ everything that anyone would want to know

15. The altimeter reading in Dr. K.'s description is an important clue because it tells _____ .

  Ⓐ the speed of the spaceship

  Ⓑ how many water molecules are in the sky

  Ⓒ the temperature outside the spaceship

  Ⓓ how high above Earth the spaceship is

16. What is wrong with Dr. K.'s description that "the moon and the stars twinkled in the blue"?

  Ⓐ Stars do not twinkle.

  Ⓑ The sky is black in space.

  Ⓒ You cannot see stars from a spaceship.

  Ⓓ You cannot see the moon from a spaceship.

17. At the end of the story, Stanley feels dejected because _____ .

(A) Dr. K. fooled him

(B) he sent Dr. K. fifty dollars

(C) Einstein kidded him

(D) Einstein solved the mystery

18. Why did the author name the main character Einstein?

(A) It is a good name for a detective.

(B) The character was named after Albert Einstein, a very smart scientist.

(C) He wanted to use the name of a famous ballplayer.

(D) He liked the sound of the name.

19. Explain briefly what Einstein thinks of Stanley's laboratory.

_____

_____

_____

_____

_____

_____

_____

20. Describe what Earth looks like from space.

_____

_____

_____

_____

_____

_____

_____